PATRICK H. CURRAN
HEDWIDGE CURRAN
1902 SH... ...AY
STOCKTON, CA 95207

S0-BUZ-115

OUR LADY COMES TO SCOTTSDALE

Is it Authentic?

by
Robert Faricy, S.J.
and
Lucy Rooney, S.N.D. de N.

Published by

The Riehle Foundation
P.O. Box 7
Milford, Ohio 45150

The publisher recognizes and accepts that the final authority regarding the apparitions at Scottsdale, Arizona rests with the Holy See of Rome, to whose judgment we willingly submit.

The Publisher

Published by The Riehle Foundation
For additional copies write to:
                    The Riehle Foundation
                    P.O. Box 7
                    Milford, OH 45150

Copyright © 1991, Robert Faricy/Lucy Rooney

Library of Congress Catalog Card No.: 91-067814

ISBN: 1-877678-20-1

All rights reserved. No part of this book may be reproduced or transmitted in any form without the written permission of the publisher. For information address The Riehle Foundation, P.O. Box 7, Milford, Ohio 45150.

COVER PHOTO By Len Zbiegien, SCULPTED By Carlos Ayala. The Blessed Sacrament Chapel at St. Maria Goretti is called "The Tabernacle." In its center is the crucifix which cradles the Hosts and which is surrounded by four adoring angels.

Table of Contents

Our Lady Comes To Scottsdale –
Is It Authentic?

St. Maria Goretti Church

Preface

Fr. Robert Faricy and Sr. Lucy Rooney have authored a number of books, with particular emphasis on the many appearances of Mary during our time. Included in their works are a number of titles on Medjugorje, Yugoslavia, a phenomena that has drawn over 15 million people to a small, remote village in Croatia. But there is much more than Medjugorje. In the past 20 years the number of claimed apparitions and supernatural messages and locutions has reached a crescendo. Why? Medjugorje, Hrushiv (Ukraine), Kibeho (Africa), in Italy, Korea, Ireland, Ecuador, Venezuela, Italy, Japan, Argentina, Egypt, to name a few, and now several reports in the United States. It is most interesting that all of the messages seem to coincide with each other, like someone is trying very desperately to get our attention.

Two years ago, the Riehle Foundation published a book titled, I AM YOUR JESUS OF MERCY. It was the first of three volumes. To date, over 300,000 copies of these volumes have been printed. They are in great demand. They contain the messages in Scottsdale, Arizona. They mirror messages received from some of the other apparition sites listed above. Like all of the above mentioned sites, these messages too cannot be disproven.

It is then important that certain credible and scholarly persons within the Church study and evaluate these events. Thus it was that Fr. Faricy and Sr. Rooney journeyed to Scottsdale, Arizona, to evaluate and interview the participants. Their complete report is included in the following pages. What they have found in Scottsdale is a reflection of all the major and credible apparition sites of our times—a tremendous current of prayer and conversion. It is an echo of the gospels.

For those who must understandably have many doubts, the gospel also establishes the criteria. When the Sanhedrin gathered to discuss how to get rid of the Apostles of Christ, Gamaliel, a teacher of the law, spoke up saying: "If this endeavor is of human origin, it will destroy itself. But if it comes from God, you will not be able to destroy them; you will find yourselves even fighting against God." (*Acts* 5:38-39).

Bill Reck
The Riehle Foundation

Introduction

We first met Annie Ross in California, at a conference about the apparitions of Our Lady going on in Medjugorje, Yugoslavia. Annie identified herself as one of two people in Scottsdale, Arizona, who regularly see and speak with Mary, the mother of Jesus. We listened to her that August evening in 1990, and then met her again four days later in Scottsdale. We had believed what Annie told us, and we went to Scottsdale to learn more about the events there.

Scottsdale, 130,000 people, lies 20 miles east of Phoenix in south central Arizona. It forms part of the two million population of the Phoenix metropolitan area. About half of this population is Catholic, with many Hispanics, especially Mexican Americans. Half the citizens of Arizona live here in the Valley of the Sun, a flat desert watered by the Colorado River, circled by sharply serrated pinkish mountains, bare except for scrub.

There are few clouds; rumor says it rains for three hours six times a year, and the rest of the time the skies are clear. Much of the land here belongs to the Pima Maricopa Indians and to the Apache Indians; Indians own over one fourth of Arizona land, and the Salt River Indian Reservation occupies a large territory just east of Scottsdale.

Since World War II, the city of Scottsdale has enjoyed prosperity, a growing population, and an important tourist industry. The homes here are mostly one story, low shady buildings, surrounded by eucalyptus and tall plumed pines, with cacti, some as tall as trees, on the lawns. Visitors come to Scottsdale, sometimes called the most western town in the west, to buy cowboy clothes in the porch-fronted stores, and for its warm and sunny winters.

In June, 1988, Mary, the mother of Jesus, allegedly began to visit Scottsdale's Saint Maria Goretti Parish to speak to some young people there. It is claimed that Jesus Himself has spoken there since August, 1988, and that beginning just after Christmas of 1989, Mary appears regularly to speak with two of these young adults.

The chapters that follow describe our experience in Scottsdale, and especially our interviews with nine young people and with the pastor of Saint Maria Goretti Parish, Father Jack Spaulding. The Catholic Church has as yet made no conclusive investigations into the Scottsdale events. Personally, as anyone can, we believe strongly in the authenticity of the Scottsdale apparitions and messages. Furthermore, as Roman Catholics we submit our observations and convictions in obedience to the Church and subject to official judgment.

Robert Faricy, SJ
Lucy Rooney, SND de N
September 15, 1991

Crucifix above the altar
St. Maria Goretti Church

Mary Cook, Fr. Spaulding, Jimmy Kupanoff

Wendy Nelson and Mary Cook

Statue of Our Lord
St. Maria Goretti Church

xi

Annie Ross and Gianna Talone

Annie Ross and Fr. Jack Spaulding

Sr. Lucy Rooney, Gianna, Fr. Robert Faricy

Susan Evans

Fr. Spaulding and James Pauley

Statue of Our Lady
St. Maria Goretti Church

CHAPTER 1

Father Jack Spaulding

Message from Our Lord given through Father Jack
during his homily, February 2, 1990.

> *My dear ones, as I sent My disciples long
> ago, I now send you. I ask you to give, once
> you have learned it here from Me, My mercy,
> totally, to those around you. I ask you to
> depend totally upon Me; not upon the gifts I
> have given you. I invite you to come often to
> Me seeking forgiveness, strength, healing.
> Come to Me in My Eucharistic presence, and
> then I will heal you, strengthen you, as you
> go back to being My disciples of mercy.*
>
> *This world needs My mercy, and I will give
> it through you My dear ones. How you have
> captured My heart! May you draw closer to
> My heart this night. And thank you for listen-
> ing. How happy you make Me when you listen
> to My words when I tell you I love you and
> am with you as you go to those to whom I
> send you.*

* * *

The pastor of Saint Maria Goretti Parish in Scottsdale
is Father Jack Spaulding. In his early forties, he is of
slight build, energetic and outgoing. He has been chan-
cellor of the diocese of Phoenix. At present, he is Vicar

1

Forane; this means that, under the bishop, he has a certain responsibility for a section of the diocese, in this case about one fourth of the diocese.

The people of the parish recognize how much he has done for the parish since becoming pastor; one parishioner who travels often says, "It is the best run parish I have seen anywhere in this country." The parish administrator, Sandra Bruner, truly administers the parish, freeing Father Jack to act as pastor and spiritual guide. The total staff of Saint Maria Goretti Parish, including the two priests, Father Spaulding and his assistant, Father Kevin McGloin, is eighteen full time persons, serving a parish of twenty six hundred families, about six thousand people, most of them active church goers. Besides pastoral workers and the parish administrator, there are secretaries and accountants, a receptionist, and a music director. Resources available to parishioners range from bible study and prayer groups to bereavement counselling, health care, teen grief support, troubled marriage help, to "Mom's spiritual support." The parish offices are a large complex. At the center of all, is the Tabernacle, a Blessed Sacrament chapel where over 700 parishioners had pledged to maintain a twenty-four hour adoration. The leader of all this is Father Jack Spaulding.

Here, in his own words, is how he has experienced the coming of Mary to his parish.

* * *

"In 1987, June, I made my first trip to Medjugorje with a priest friend, Father Dale Fushek, and our television crew. Father Dale and I do a weekly national cable television show for teenagers, called the *Life Teen Program*. It is on Mother Angelica's network out of Birmingham, Alabama, the Eternal Word Television Network (EWTN).

"Dale and I went over there for the anniversary, June

25, 1987. We believed before we went. We were able to
be in the rectory where our Blessed Mother was
appearing in one of the priests' offices.

"Later that year, in October 1987, I took about
ninety-five parishioners, including some teenagers and
some young adults. When we got back the teenagers
decided to form a prayer group. They have had it on
and off for almost three years. Just recently they re-
established the group to put it on another night. About
twenty high school kids come and pray together for an
hour and a half on Monday nights. They have the
Rosary, shared prayer, and then if anyone wants prayer
they pray with each other.

"In October the adults came to me and said, "Can
we have a prayer group?" I said, "Go ahead. But the
only thing I would ask you is not to have it be a 'Medjugorje group' type of thing. Let it be for anyone in the
parish." So they did.

"On Thursday, December 3, 1987, we began the adult
prayer group at Saint Maria Goretti. There were about
twenty or thirty adults. Now there are over five hundred most of the time. They wanted to pray fifteen
decades of the Rosary and have Mass, exactly as they
do at Medjugorje.

"I went back to Medjugorje in March '88 to do
another television special, this time with our local CBS
affiliate. And in June '88 I went back with a group of
parishioners. One of the young adults who had come
to the prayer group, Gianna Talone, and her mother
went with us. Wayne Weible [an internationally known
writer and speaker about the events at Medjugorje] was
there. He was giving a talk. Gianna went to meet him
after his presentation. Wayne tells it this way: he was
attracted to Gianna as she was coming up, and went
to her and said, 'You are going to play a very significant

role in Our Lady's plan. Gianna looked at him. She had never met the man. She said, 'OK.'

"The next day she came to me and said, 'Father, I think the Blessed Mother spoke to me.' I thought, 'Oh, here we go again!' She went to Wayne. He tells it this way, 'She came up to me and said, 'I think the Blessed Mother spoke to me.' The first thing I thought was, 'What did I start! I told the woman she was going to have a significant role to play in the Blessed Mother's plan, and now she is hearing her voice!' So I asked Gianna what it was that Our Lady said. It was a very basic thing. 'Come closer to my Son and pray, pray, pray.'

"We came home, and Gianna started coming to me. I had seen her at the prayer group but I really didn't know her very well. I remembered blessing her condominium. So messages began coming. I started to use the basic criteria that the Church always uses when faced with these special kinds of gifts. These are: Is the individual being drawn closer to the Sacrament of Reconciliation and the Sacrament of the Eucharist? Is the person changing behavior in their life that perhaps needs to be changed? Is the message itself in accord with scripture, or at least not contradicting it? Is it in accord with what we have always believed as Catholic Christians in our tradition? Lastly, is the person being drawn out of themselves to serve other people? I was able to answer, or she was able to answer, 'yes' to all of those things.

"Another young adult came to me about a week later—Stefanie. Stefanie is a brilliant young woman of about twenty-seven. She works with accounting firms. She is very brilliant, straight forward, didn't go to church very much, but started to come to our prayer group. I had seen her around. She came in one day and said exactly the same as Gianna did at the very beginning, 'I think I am going crazy Father. I am hearing a voice.' She receives messages a bit differently from Gianna. At the very beginning she received long treatises. As far as religion goes, Stefanie hadn't a clue, nor had she any theological background to have written these things herself. She was anxious and concerned about them. She handed me this and said: 'This voice said this. I didn't.' After I read it I knew she didn't say it. She couldn't know what it was. It was about conversion of heart, and it was one of the most beautifully theological and pastoral treatises that I have ever read on what converting your heart meant.

"About a week later another young adult came in. Steve is a great guy. He is a rodeo person. He ropes. He said: 'Father I think I am going crazy.' I said, 'Steve, let me finish the sentence for you!. . . It was a lady's voice saying very simple things like "Come to my Son."' His question to me was, 'Does that mean I have to be a priest?' I said, 'Did she ask you to be a priest, Steve?' He said, 'No.' So I said, 'Don't do anything she doesn't say.' Then he asked, 'Will she ask me to give up my roping?' I said, 'I don't know—has she asked you?. . .Then don't.' Eight months later he came in and he said, 'She has asked me to give up my roping. . . .She can have anything she wants.'

"I asked Steve and the others to keep quiet about things, so that they did not compare notes or influence each other. I also asked them to keep a journal, and I know that some of them do, especially Stefanie, Gianna and Annie, and possibly Mary.

"I cannot remember if Steve or his sister Wendy came to me first. Wendy does not hear a voice most of the time—it is an inner thing. She has had a real conversion. She is a strong person once she has made up her mind. She is obedient too when Jesus or Mary ask something of her.

"Susan had started converting before any of the others. I was her spiritual director. She does not necessarily hear a voice, but feels an interior urging. All the kids are converting, changing their way of life. Their jobs were the center, now their jobs are just to pay their bills.

"Jimmy was the last of the original six. He fought it for a long time. I knew him best because he had lived at the rectory for a while when his family moved away. Jimmy finally said 'yes.' He hears a voice sometimes, but usually it is a burning in his heart.

"In August of '88 I went back to Medjugorje for the feast of the Assumption at the end of the Marian year. That is when things started to happen with me; I couldn't explain them too well until I got back home and sat down with my spiritual director. I was walking in one of the fields in Medjugorje, the one that leads from the church to Vicka's house. I was alone. I would like to say that I was praying fervently. I wasn't. I was thinking of nothing in particular.

"All of a sudden I heard a voice saying to me: 'You are to walk by faith and not by sight.' I looked around—nobody was there, so I knew who it was because it was a voice.

"On August 15 I was concelebrating the English speaking Mass. I was so distracted. It was August 15, the end of the Marian year, the feast of the Assumption—people were in and out of that church taking snap shots. We were sweating. There was no air conditioning. It was terrible. After I received Holy Communion I sat down waiting for everyone else to finish and I was talking to Our Lady, saying, 'Dear Lady, you just can't be here any more. Look at these people, look at this—they have turned it into a carnival. You just can't be here still.' I heard a voice, very clear, saying to me, 'I am here, and I am going home with you.' I didn't know what that meant until I got home and all these things started.

"Other young adults were sent to me, nine of them now. At that point there were only six. Gianna and Stefanie came to me to say that Our Lady would ask Mary Cook. I had known Mary briefly, but her family had moved back to Wisconsin. Gianna knew her slightly, Stefanie better. Both said Mary had said 'no,' but Our Lady would ask her again. If she said 'yes,' she would be back in Scottsdale again. The very next week when I looked at my appointment book, there was her name. When we met, she had the same look on her face as Gianna and Stefanie had, and she said the same thing, 'I think I am going crazy. . .a voice inviting me to come back here and talk to you. I said "no," then I said "yes."'

"Jimmy Kupanoff said 'yes' at first, then 'no,' and went away. He came back, and said to me, 'Gee, Father Jack, I really would like that to happen to me.' I answered him, 'Hasn't it already? The only thing to do is to say "yes."'

"Annie was the last of the nine to come. I knew her well, and was more skeptical about her than about the others. Some of the criteria for evaluation did not fit her at first. They do now.

"On September 16, the day after the feast of the 'Exaltation of the Holy Cross and Mother of Sorrows,' the young adults asked if they could start a prayer group. The young adults are anybody out of high school, and up to thirty-two or thirty-three. They began with a group of about seventeen, meeting on Friday nights. They meet for an hour and a half and pray specifically for the conversion of the young adults of America. That is what Our Lady and Our Lord have asked us to do. We pray the Chaplet of Mercy, then the Sorrowful mysteries, then we pray spontaneously.

"In July of '88, after the Thursday adult prayer group was over, Gianna came up to me. She said, 'I think I am going crazy.' I said, 'Gianna you already told me that. What now?' She said: 'I think I have received a message for the parish.' I thought. . .'Not just private ones; now public ones! What am I going to do with this?' I asked her, 'What was it?' She told me. It was very beautiful. I was still skeptical, thinking that she was caught up in the messages of Medjugorje. I did a check on her. She wasn't familiar with the messages from Medjugorje. From that time on Gianna would receive the message during the prayer group on Thursday evening, write it down, give it to me and I would read it the following week to the people before we began to pray.

"Around October that year, or early November, she came up as she usually did to give me the message. She said, 'Here is the second half of the message Father.' I said, 'Thank you. Where is the first half?' 'Well,' she said, 'the Blessed Mother told me that you covered it pretty well in your homily.'

"In November I remember getting up in front of the altar, at the prayer group Mass, to give a homily, and going completely blank. I didn't not only not remember what I was going to say in the homily, I didn't even remember what the gospel was that had just been proclaimed by the deacon. I didn't know who I was! A feeling came over me like I was being drained. All of a sudden I heard myself speaking. And it wasn't me speaking. It lasted about forty-five seconds. Then it was over. And I don't even remember hearing what it was. I just remember when it was over I was so tired that I could hardly make it back up to where I was sitting. I had to wait until I could get up and continue the Mass.

"I finished the Mass and caught sight of Gianna

afterwards. She told me that Our Lady had said to her she does not want her children to have to wait for a week to hear what she has to say to them. 'If you will say "yes," she will use you like this every now and then.' So that is what has been happening at the Thursday night prayer group every now and then. More now, than then, but it does not happen every Thursday.

"Toward December that same feeling started just before the gospel reading. Only it was a different feeling; a lot stronger and my whole body tingled. I went out in front and it started, only this time it wasn't Our Lady speaking. It was Our Lord. I don't beg you to believe this. I just know what I know, and that is what happened. The best way I can explain it: it is as if Our Lady or Our Lord at that time used me as I am using this microphone. I don't hear the words before. It just comes out. It is not very long, about forty-five seconds or a minute. It is certainly not my style. It is very simple, direct, and sometimes almost an emotionless voice; other times there is more emotion. People who have taped it say that the voice changes between Our Lord and Our Lady. Sometimes I hear what is being said, but mostly not, or not all of it. I think that it is different from prophecy in the charismatic renewal movement.

"During Lent, not this year but last [1989], Our Lord and Our Lady told us we would not be receiving messages like that, that they wanted us to offer Lent up for the salvation of souls. I tried to make it happen, to make the feeling inside myself happen. I just can't do it.

"The bishop formed a commission. Their findings are like the findings usually are of any commission that the diocese or the Church sets up: that, first of all, there is no proof of supernatural or miraculous happenings here. But there could be such happenings. So they recommend that the prayer group continue. As I told the bishop and the commission, we started the prayer group in December 1987. The messages didn't begin until July '88.

"The great majority of people come to pray, not to listen to the message, because they don't know, as we don't, if there is going to be a message. The young adults and I know this, that we can say 'no.' God, Our Lady, never, never, interferes with our free will, ever. They always invite. Even when they admonish us— even that is done in a gentle way. Every now and then they ask us, 'Do you want to continue to say 'yes?' If you want to say 'no' we won't love you any less, but we will ask someone else.' If we don't listen, they stop speaking, not as a punishment, but so as not to interfere with free will. We know none of this is happening because of our holiness or any good things we have done. It only has to do with us saying 'yes.'

"A year and a half ago, one of the messages Gianna received was, 'I will appear to you and then to the others.' It didn't happen. That started all kinds of doubts in my mind and my heart, because the messages were right on. What they are showing us is that it is not in our time, it is in their time.

"The latter part of December '89, Our Lady started to appear to Gianna. She appears to her every day and during the prayer group on Thursday evenings. Now she has appeared to four of the nine. So the others are waiting.

"One of the great things that has been happening is that each of the nine have come to me and said: 'Father, the most important thing, the most valuable, and the greatest gift is not receiving the messages or even seeing Our Lady. It is the conversion of heart that is continuing to take place.' Most of the messages they receive are for their personal growth and conversion.

I have come to realize that there are at least two conversions. The first is conversion of life—we have some control over that as it continues on: changing behavior, changing attitudes. Real conversion, conversion of heart—over that we have no control except to say 'yes' to the Lord. The Lord is the one who does that in His time and in His way. Most of the time it is not how we would do it!

"In September 1988 Gianna came to me again and said, 'Our Lord is giving me these lessons.' She gave me the first few. I couldn't believe it. She is wonderfully simple; she said, 'Our Lord wants them published for the world.'

"Each one of us has been given a symbol by Our Lord. I don't know what exactly they mean. There are ten: Truth, Faith, Strength, Joy, Compassion, Humility, Courage, Hope, Mercy, Love and Charity. They are all virtues of Jesus' heart.

"Our Lady told us she will be with us at Maria Goretti in a special way for three years. She has asked for a three year commitment from the nine and myself. She has asked us to give up our future—to let Them give us our future. If the devil can make us guilty about the past and worried about their future, we will never experience God, because God isn't in the past, and isn't in the future, he is right here. What They want us to do is live in the present.

"She has said to us that she has come to America to meet the devil on his own ground. If we yuppies in Scottsdale can with God's help convert our hearts, anybody can. The kids kid around—that they have committed every sin in the book. So anybody who comes can't say, 'Oh you were always so holy.' No, they weren't. I knew them before, and they knew me before. So it has nothing to do with what happened before, and it has everything to do with us saying 'yes.' She has said to us that she has come to America to meet the devil on his own ground.

"Gianna and Annie, and Wendy and Mary, the four girls who have seen her, say that she comes out of the statue. First of all the statue glows, then turns into a human person, then she comes out of it. Then she looks nothing like the statue. She comes as *Our Lady of Joy.* She is dressed in dazzling white. She has dark hair and brilliant blue eyes. They say she is beautiful beyond words. She is between eighteen and twenty-five. Recently she came with her arms outstretched, and in her arms were countless long stemmed white roses without any thorns on them. And she said: *These are your prayers which you are offering to my Son. They make me so joyful. I am your Lady of Joy.*"

* * *

In the fall of 1988, Our Lady supposedly told Gianna that she and Jesus wanted to speak directly to the assembly on Thursday night at the prayer group, and that Father Jack would have the option to refuse if he wanted to. Mary added that our free will is a great gift, and that God always waits for us to say, "yes." Father Jack said "yes," and he says "yes" every Thursday evening that he goes into the pulpit after the reading of the gospel and feels that Jesus or Mary wants to speak through him. He never knows in advance, and is always ready to give a homily on the readings of the Mass of that day. During the reading of the gospel, They let him know whether or not They want to speak through him right after the gospel instead of giving a homily.

I asked Father Spaulding how he feels during the reading of the gospel at the Thursday night Mass, and what happens. He told me this:

"You asked me about Thursday evenings during the homily. The best I can say is that it doesn't happen all

Thursdays, only some Thursdays, more Thursdays
than not, but I never know whether it's going to happen or not until maybe a few minutes before, usually
during the readings, either the first reading or the second reading. This sensation comes over me, so that I
know that Our Lord wants to speak. When that happens, then He uses me—the best way that I can explain
it—He uses me the way that I would a microphone. I
don't know what He's going to say before He says it;
I just start it. And it lasts maybe forty-five seconds or
a minute; it doesn't last very long at all. When He fin-
ishes, that's it; I go back and sit down. Sometimes it
happens, when He doesn't speak through me, that I
know what He wants me to say, so I say it, but just
in my own words. But it doesn't happen all the time.
In Lent of 1989, Our Lord and Our Lady both told us
that They wouldn't speak to us, that They wanted us
to concentrate on sacrifice and prayer. So, during that
time, I tried to get the feeling that it's going to happen,
and it doesn't work. I wanted to see if I'm just making
this up or not. And it doesn't work. I know that I can
say 'no'. . .They never interfere with our free will, it's
always if we will.

"One time there were people I knew, visiting, in the
congregation. I didn't want it to happen, but I felt it
coming. I said 'no' and the feeling passed. Then I said,
'Lord do as you wish.' It happened.

"Jesus speaks in the first person. Many times He
says, *I am your Jesus of mercy,* . . . Sometimes it's Our
Lady. Very seldom lately it's Our Lady. And I know the
difference, because when it's Our Lady who wants to
speak, it's much gentler."

Father Jack has told us that his difficulty in all these
events was that they were out of his control. He says,
"I was anxious for the kids, that they were OK; I
wanted to spare their feelings. I wanted to make

excuses for Our Lord and Our Lady! From the beginning I knew this was bigger than I could control or handle. My spiritual director is open and discerning. He is steeped in the early Fathers. He says, 'Who are we to say that God can or can't act?' We have to allow things to unfold in Their timing. But I had been praying: 'Lord, help me to understand'—by which I meant, 'Lord help **me** to control.' All of us see that what is asked of us is the 'yes' of obedience—the kind of obedience Our Lord has, blind, just saying 'yes.'"

* * *

Message from Our Lady given through Father Jack during his homily March 22, 1990.

> *My dear children, I your mother come to you tonight and, as your mother, I ask you to listen to what my Son Jesus tells you. Our Father allows Us to be with you and to be closer to Him always. I ask you, my dear ones, to devote yourselves more and more to prayer. I know, my dear ones that you feel lonely these days. Please do not think that I, your mother abandoned you, and that my Son Jesus does not walk with you any longer. We are still with you. Bear the sacrifice of loneliness. I am here tonight to tell you again, that We are always with you; always near you; always in your heart. Continue on in these days to honor my Son, responding to His grace, His call.*
>
> *My dear children, listen to Him speaking to your heart, and allow His Spirit to fill you with peace. I love you and take you into my arms and hold you close to my heart!*

Message from Our Lady given through Father Jack during his homily January 31, 1991:

My dear ones, I ask you to listen to me with your hearts. I have been asking this for countless generations. I your mother, thank you for listening. My dear, dear children, I see your sorrow and I take that sorrow and present it to God Our Father. And through my Son Jesus, Our Father gives you back hope. I am with you. This is the reason for your hope. I ask you again this night, with love, to pray. You and I join in prayer that the gift of hope which my Son brings to you, will be accepted by the world. I am with you. I love you and take you to my heart. I present you this night to my Son, and We together present you to God Our Father. Thank you for listening. Be my hope-filled children.

Message from Jesus, given through Father Jack during his homily, February 7, 1991.

My dear ones, I do not want you to be far from Me, and I, your Jesus of Mercy, am never far from you. My dear children, you are not alone. The Spirit of My Father and Myself is within you. Please do not run from Me. I want to take you in My arms. I see how often you are in pain. If you allow Me to take you, I will bring you through that pain into true love and joy. I ask you: come nearer to Me; nearer each day until you come into My heart. My dear ones, as My heart was opened by the lance as I hung on the cross, that opening is for you. I love you and I ask you not to fear. I am here with you always. I give you peace that you need at this moment. I shed My mercy upon you My beloved children.

Message from Jesus given through Father Jack during his homily, March 14, 1991:

> *My dear people, My dear ones! I ask you this night to turn again to the road of mercy. You have not been merciful. I ask you to strive not to judge. I see your heart; and I see how you are trying, but I also see how easy it is for you to allow your heart to grow cold and to become hardened. My dear ones, I want to take you in My arms. When you are not merciful, you prevent Me from embracing you as I wish. Each of you is My disciple of mercy. I love you! I ask you not to give up. I do not give up on you.*

Message from Jesus given through Father Jack, during his homily, August 15, 1991:

> *My dear ones, I, your Jesus of Mercy, tell you this night that My mother is the queen of My heart, because it was from her heart that Our Holy Spirit formed My heart. My dear ones, as you honor her, you honor Me and you give glory to Our Father. Words, human words, cannot even begin to phrase the love that I have for her. She is MY MOTHER. I love her. I ask you to love her also. She so much wants you as her dearest children. She tells God Our Father that she sees Me in all of you. That is how much she loves you. Love her. Run to her before you are lost. Again this night My dear ones, I give you My mother. Cherish her as I cherish her, and she will lead you, not only to Me, but to God Our Father. Peace My dear ones! Peace to you.*

CHAPTER 2

Gianna

Message from Our Lady to the Parish, given through Gianna, June 28, 1990:

> *My dear children, seek my Jesus with all your heart. Give to Him all of your love. This above all, is the greatest gift you could give to my Son. Love Him totally and do not expect anything other than His love in return. He has given you many gifts and will continue to give to you all good things. My wish for you tonight is for you to love my Son, your Savior, with all of your heart. Thank you my dear ones for responding to my call.*

*   *   *

The story of Jesus and Mary visiting Scottsdale in a special way, begins with Doctor Gianna Talone. Gianna began to hear Our Lady speaking to her on June 4, 1988, at Medjugorje, Yugoslavia, where Mary appears to a small group of young adults. At the end of 1989, Our Lady apparently began to appear to Gianna as well as to speak with her—at least once a day, usually in the evening, and sometimes also during the day if she has something urgent or especially important to tell Gianna. She asked Gianna for the sacrifice of not seeing her on Fridays. Since late 1988, Gianna claims Jesus has appeared to her a few times, and speaks with her on an almost daily basis, usually several times a day.

Gianna Talone, born in March 1957, was married for some years to Michael Bianchi, a commercial artist and graphic designer. They had no children, and in early 1991 Michael left her, filing for divorce. The marriage has been annulled. Gianna holds a doctoral degree in Pharmacy. She has worked in a management position for a major pharmaceutical company as well as in a pharmacy preparing prescriptions. She now works as clinical pharmacologist and pharmacy coordinator at Saint Joseph's Hospital in Phoenix, run by the Sisters of Mercy, a work in which she finds much happiness. Gianna is petite, dark, attractive, with luminous brown eyes and great warmth.

The fall of 1987 marks the beginning of the visits of Jesus and Mary to Scottsdale. In Gianna's own words:

"In September 1987, I had a dream of Our Blessed Mother, three nights in a row, and every night it was the same dream. The dream was that I was sleeping in my room and Our Lady came and stood next to my bed praying over me. In the dream I knew I was sleeping, but my eyes were open and I saw Our Lady. I was awakened from my sleep to see Our Lady. She was beautiful, but did not say anything. She only smiled and prayed for me.

"She looked in the dream exactly as I see her now. Dark hair, steel blue eyes, rosy cheeks and lips, perfect porcelain white complexion, long fingers, slim, wearing a white robe with a white veil (not a heavy cloth, but a veil). At first I thought: this is the best dream I've ever had. The next night I had the same dream, and the night following I had the same identical dream. I knew then it wasn't a dream but that Our Lady had come to me while Michael and I were sleep-

ing, and I awoke to see her. This is what she told me
later. I told only my mother at that point because I had
not a clue what it all meant.

"Then, in November 1987, I was in Saint Maria
Goretti's church praying on my lunch hour when the
angel Saint Gabriel came to me. I never used to go to
church on my lunch hour, but after my dream I began
to have an incredible desire for Eucharist daily and to
pray the Rosary.

"Anyway, this one afternoon in November, I had just
finished saying my prayers and was getting ready to
go back to work when I could not get up from the
kneeler. A force was on my left shoulder and I heard
a male voice say, 'The Lord seeks favor upon you for
you have cried for the Lord. You will do great things.'
I was alone in the church and was troubled by those
words. I didn't tell anyone except my mother because
I thought it was a personal thing. Later Our Lord told
me He had sent Saint Gabriel to tell me that message
because he is sent to bring tidings of joy."

In June 1988, Gianna, while praying to Our Lady,
asked to go to Medjugorje to see her. Within a week
Gianna received a paid vacation and, also, the last
available seat on the plane she wanted to take to Yugoslavia. Our Lady began to speak to Gianna on June 4
in Medjugorje.

"I did not see her, but I heard her. She said, 'Your
prayers give glory to God. Please do not pray for yourself. Pray for others who suffer so the Lord will bless
them, and pray for peace in souls, in families, and in
the world. Don't be fearful, for I will protect and guide
you. If you do this, I will bless you with health and
prosperity.' On June 6, 1988, she said, 'People do not
pray with their hearts. They do not give praise and
glory to Jesus when things are going well for them.'"
Our Lady spoke to Gianna each day in Medjugorje,

from June 4th through June 10th.

On June 6th Gianna claimed a vision of the infant Jesus. Later, Mary told her that Jesus only presents Himself as a child when He is in joy with someone. She said that Jesus was joyful with Gianna because she was childlike. "After this," Gianna says, "Our Lady sent me to Vicka for confirmation that my messages were from Our Lady."

On June 8th Gianna met with Vicka Ivankovic, one of the four people in their twenties, two women and two men, in the parish of Saint James at Medjugorje, each of whom has seen and spoken with Our Lady nearly every day since June, 1981. Vicka confirmed that Gianna's messages were truly from Our Lady, and told Gianna to open her heart and to listen for other messages to come.

At that time, Gianna spoke of all this to no one except her mother. Later, when Our Lady advised her that she could, she told others what had happened. Our Lady continued to speak daily to Gianna when she returned to Scottsdale, and sent her to tell her pastor, Father Jack Spaulding, one of the two priests of Saint Maria Goretti Parish. He questioned her closely about her spiritual experience and about her personal relationships. After Medjugorje, Gianna's life was not the same. Her family said she was a different person. Especially, she had a great thirst for prayer.

Gianna claims that on July 14, 1988, Mary gave her the first of the weekly messages for Saint Maria Goretti Parish. These messages have continued to come every week at the Thursday night prayer meeting in the church of Saint Maria Goretti. The Thursday night prayer meeting began in late 1987 after a group of parishioners, who had been to Medjugorje, asked Father Spaulding, the parish pastor, to start it. About twenty people met every Thursday evening to say the fifteen decades of the Rosary together, to have Mass after the Rosary, and then to have healing prayer. The schedule follows generally, the evening order at Saint James Parish in Medjugorje.

Eventually more people came. By the fall of 1990 between four and six hundred people came to the prayer meeting, many of them young people. Father Spaulding says the Mass and preaches. Eventually the Chaplet of Mercy of the Polish Sister Faustina began to be substituted for the Sorrowful Mysteries of the Rosary. Now, the congregation begins the meeting with the Joyful Mysteries, then recites the Chaplet of Mercy—a rosary-like prayer. Mass follows, then the Glorious Mysteries of the Rosary and prayers for healing.

At some point during the five Joyful Mysteries, Our Lady apparently appears to both Gianna and Annie Ross, and she gives Gianna a message for the parish. Annie also sees Our Lady, speaks with her, and hears the message.

We sat in one of the front rows, beside Gianna and Annie, for a Thursday evening prayer meeting. Over five hundred persons attended, over half of them young, under thirty-five. We learned later that only about one hundred or so are from Scottsdale. The others came from out of town, some from California and Texas, even from Mexico.

Both young women prayed in a fairly common Catholic position, half sitting and half kneeling. At the beginning of the third *Hail Mary* of the second Joyful Mystery, *Mary Visits Her Cousin Elizabeth*, both Gianna and Annie in perfect simultaneity knelt straight, their eyes fixed on a point near the statue of Our Lady standing in the left front of the church. They stayed that way until the tenth *Hail Mary* of the fourth Joyful Mystery.

They were both clearly in ecstasy, totally oblivious to their surroundings, entirely focused on something no one else could see or hear. Both had radiant expressions. Their lips and vocal cords moved, but we could not hear anything they said. They often nodded or smiled. They looked like they were conversing with an unseen third party. It reminded us a lot of the apparitions at Medjugorje in Yugoslavia.

They told us that the apparitions can last from a minute up to several minutes. Carol Ameche, who types up the messages and keeps a record of them, says this: "One night we saw Gianna and Annie stand up toward the end of the apparition. You can tell when it begins because they kneel up straight and they move in absolute synchrony. There is no way you could fake that—no way. I never saw anything like it. They are kneeling upright, and they are looking in one spot, and sometimes—their faces are always radiant—sometimes there is joy, sometimes they look sad, and sometimes they look serious. This night they stood up and took turns standing on their tip toes and raising their heads. They told us later that Our Lady had come down and kissed them on the forehead. That story is important that we know and realize that Our Lady is real flesh and blood. That is how Our Lady is appearing. She went to Heaven body and soul, and she is coming back to us the same way. So they have embraced her; she has hugged them; she has kissed them; they have kissed her. A very close motherly relationship has developed with them—but with all of us. She is so concerned and so loving and so motherly—it is wonderful."

Gianna and Annie told us later that Our Lady seems to step out of the statue. They both see and hear her quite clearly. They see her surrounded by light. She has a great and shining radiance; she is beautiful, and there is light all around her. She usually wears a grey gown and a white veil. She has dark hair, blue eyes, beautiful skin.

Mary speaks a message to Gianna; Annie hears the message, and corroborates it afterward. After the prayer meeting, Gianna gives the message, now written down, to the pastor, and he reads it at the next meeting without any special introduction. It seems unlikely that many in the church are aware of the real origin of the message read to them. In fact, when Gianna and Annie go into ecstasy during the recitation of the Rosary, no one seems to notice it nor perceive that something special has begun to take place. We found no emphasis either on the apparitions or on the message. The point of the prayer meeting is **prayer**.

In fact, it seems doubtful that all those present are even aware that apparitions apparently take place or that the message read comes straight from the Mother of God. Under orders from the bishop, these things are not preached. Much of the congregation is from outside the parish. Probably many in the parish do not even know, or know only vaguely, about Mary's visitation of their parish.

On August 10, 1988, Gianna claimed her first message from Jesus. "I was at work. Our Lord said, 'My child, know that you are never alone. I am in you, and you are in Me. We are one in each other. My Spirit lives in you and gives you strength, wisdom and love. All the things you do give honor and praise to My Father because I am in you and My Spirit is in you and you dwell in My House.' I did not see Our Lord; I only heard Him."

He continues to speak to Gianna, saying, for example on August 22, 1991: . . .*Take hold of your new beginning. For when I bleed, so shall you. When I weep, so shall you. When I laugh, so shall you. When I shed My mercy, so shall you. When I am joyful through the bliss of My love, your love shall radiate.* The new beginning may refer to Our Lady's sending Gianna to Rome in the fall of 1991. She told Gianna that a new phase of her life would begin in Rome. Echoing Jesus' words, the Blessed Mother has warned Gianna: "You will bleed soon." Our Lord said on August 19, 1991; *I have revealed to you the depths of My intimate love and of My wounds. . . Be careful with your words so as not to open My wounds when I come to you to dress them with your love.*

Gianna is not the only one among the nine to experience physically, the pain of the wounds of Jesus. One day in August 1991, Gianna was overwhelmed by physical pain and interior darkness. As she waited for Our Lady to come that evening she had decided to say that she could take no more. Our Lady came, and as Gianna describes it: "She recommitted me to Our Lord. We said a prayer together. Here I was, planning to bail out, and I ended up recommitting. Our Lady has a certain convincing loving way!"

Mary continued to speak to Gianna every day. And, on September 20, 1988, Jesus began to dictate lessons to Gianna daily. He means these lessons for everyone, for the world. He has promised six sets of lessons. So far, Gianna has received five. Each lesson has a separate theme. For example, in a long lesson on "Difficulties," Jesus said, May 7, 1990:

> *I am your source of joy, peace and strength. I care for you even in your difficulties. I never said that if you follow Me, there would not be any difficulties for you to face. My walk is not always an easy walk, but it is a peaceful one if you totally trust in Me and in My care. . . . I tell you that you desire Me, but*

*you desire a plan that **you** have designed for
your life. . . .This results in your struggle
with difficulties. . .Will you trust in My care
by accepting with humility My plan for you?
When you accept yourselves by accepting Me,
you will be filled with My peace and strength
to face endless difficulties.*

Gianna told us that her favorite lesson from Our
Lord is the one on "Discipleship," which He gave her
on May 21, 1990. In it Jesus amplifies ten steps
towards faithful discipleship. He names the ten steps
as:

1. Put your trust in Me, your Lord God. . .
2. Never be self-righteous. . .
3. Always pray that My Father's will be
   done, and accept it with open hearts. . .
4. Rejoice in Me. . .
5. Never worry. . .
6. Love unconditionally. . .
7. Never give up hope. . .
8. Carry your cross. . .
9. Seek the kingdom of God. . .
10. Always be honest. . .

Jesus adds that He has come to restore to everyone, dignity and respect through His mercy.

On December 28, 1988, Jesus appeared to Gianna as
the Sacred Heart. "Our Lord appeared to me as the
Sacred Heart of Jesus. I was at home, and He said, 'I
am your Jesus of Mercy.' He was incredibly handsome.
His eyes were brown; His hair was wavy and around
shoulder length. He was wearing a white linen robe
with a rope-like sash around His waist. I saw these
bright gold and white rays shooting out from His heart.

I was almost blinded. I could barely see His heart. His hands were extended towards me."

Up until August of 1991, when we last spoke with her, Gianna has seen Jesus only twice although He speaks to her often. She remains in a nearly continuous personal contact with Him. About a year after she first saw Jesus, Our Lady began to appear to Gianna, on December 19, 1989.

"When I first saw her, I was praying, and I was frightened. I got my holy water and sprinkled it on her and told her to go away if she was not of God. She smiled at me and said, 'Praised be my Son, Jesus.' Afterwards I ran to the kitchen where Michael was and began crying. He got startled and said: 'What's wrong?' I told him Our Lady appeared, and he hugged me and said: 'Well don't cry. Tell me what she looks like.'"

Our Lady apparently has come to Gianna every day since then, with the exception of Fridays. She has asked Gianna to do penance for Jesus on Fridays, and so Mary does not appear to her on those days.

Gianna says, "There was even a period of forty days that Our Lady asked me for penance for Our Lord, that They would not speak to me. This was in 1988, before I even saw Our Lady, but it was very difficult for me then, not hearing her. She gave me three days to answer. So sometimes she asks me things of this nature for Our Lord."

The period of forty days was Lent of 1989. During this Lenten season, Gianna suffered much. She says that Lent was "nothing but hard labor." Earlier, on December 28, 1988 Jesus had told her she would resign from her management post in a pharmaceutical company before the end of the year. The next day, she did, with considerable suffering. She then went to work in the local Walgreens drugstore, in a shopping center two blocks from the church. Gianna worked there for three months as a retail pharmacist, a job far below her qualifications and capacity, and with a gruelling schedule. She began this work just before Lent, when Jesus and Mary did not speak to her. She shared her sufferings with her mother, who suggested she pray to Saint Joseph, since not conversing with the saints was not part of the penance. Gianna prayed to Saint Joseph.

And Saint Joseph spoke to her, assuring her of his intercessory prayers. "I prayed to Saint Joseph, and he said to me, 'My dear one, I would be happy to intercede for you. I will begin praying now.' "

A week later Gianna telephoned Saint Joseph's Hospital. She works there now, as a clinical pharmacist and pharmacy coordinator. At Saint Joseph's request, she says daily, for his intentions, one *Our Father*, one *Hail Mary*, and one *Glory be*.

Gianna has received some secrets from the Lord, secrets about events of which He has not allowed her to speak. Some of these events have already come about, and Gianna, as instructed by Jesus, has told a priest before-hand. Jesus has told her that she does not yet have all the secrets He will give her. In August 1991 Gianna received an eighth secret, this time from Our Lady. The previous ones had been given to her by Our Lord. Gianna does not know, of course, whether or not her secrets are the same ones given to the young people at Medjugorje.

Although Gianna had seen Jesus only three times up to the fall of 1991, He communicates with her frequently, and in three different ways. He speaks with her directly, as one person to another. In a second mode of communication, the Lord seems to lift her soul or her spirit out of her body, "and instantly I have this knowledge." Jesus has told Gianna that this is the purest mode of communication, because it does not permit misinterpretation. It is immediate knowledge, often of what it might have taken five or ten minutes to listen to and to write down.

The third way that Jesus communicates with Gianna is when she sleeps. "My spirit leaves. Our Lord takes me places to pray. I find myself at the bedside of someone in anguish, praying for that person, for example. And I wake up in the morning exhausted."

Gianna sees Our Lady every day except Fridays, at least once, and converses with her often during the day. Our Lady has taught her, for example, about death, Heaven, and Hell. And about this book, telling Gianna that she, Mary, wants us to write it, and that it will be published.

The Lord has given Gianna much: graces and gifts. She can often read people's intentions, for example, knowing whether their intentions are good or bad. Jesus has told her that she needs to warn those whom she knows are not on the way to salvation. If she tells them and they are not converted, then that is not her fault. But if she does not warn them, then she will be responsible for the loss of those souls, because she did not warn them. The devil attacks Gianna, often at night. She can wake up with bruises on her body. Jesus has told her that this is for purposes of redemption, to help others to be saved, and for Gianna's own greater strength. Gianna goes to Mass every day, spends much time in prayer, and receives spiritual direction from Father Ernest Larkin, a well-known Carmelite theologian and spiritual director.

Gianna's husband, Michael Bianchi, left her in early 1991; that same year he sued for divorce, and the marrige was annulled by the Church. This has been, and continues to be, a terrible cross for Gianna, deeply in love with her husband.

The last time that we saw Gianna before finishing

this book we were all together, Gianna, Sister Lucy
Rooney, and Father Robert Faricy, at the annual Catholic Charismatic Convention the last weekend of August,
1991, at the Anaheim Convention Center, south of Los
Angeles. Jesus had said to Gianna Saturday morning
that, during Father Faricy's workshop in the afternoon,
He would replace Father Faricy with Gianna. Well over
three thousand people packed a large hall for the
workshop on praying for the Holy Spirit. After giving
an introduction and beginning to pray for the Holy
Spirit, Father Faricy became quite ill and was forced
to leave the hall. Sister Lucy came to the microphone
to lead the prayer. But the Lord worked through
Gianna.

After praying first at the microphone, she moved
among the large crowd, praying over individuals,
really only touching them briefly. As soon as they were
touched, almost all immediately fell to the floor overcome by grace.

Sunday morning, at a workshop on the Blessed Virgin Mary, after Father Faricy finished speaking, Gianna
again prayed first at the microphone and then went
down off the stage to pray with individual persons. The
same thing happened, perhaps even more dramati-
cally. Many healings, both inner healings and physical
healings, have been reported from the two workshops,
although none have been verified.

After the Sunday morning workshop, the three of us,
Sister Lucy, Father Faricy, and Gianna, led the Rosary
in another large hall at the Convention Center. At the
end of the Rosary, Our Lady told Gianna that she was
coming. Gianna had her regular daily apparition, not
in the evening in private, but publicly, a little after
noon, in front of over three thousand people.

Gianna is not alone in Scottsdale in having a special
relationship with Jesus and Mary. Eight other young

people have some kind of involvement, in different ways and to different degrees, in the Scottsdale events. Towards the end of June 1988, Gianna had a vision. In the vision, she saw six young adults kneeling, seeing Our Lady, Gianna herself was one of the people in her vision; the others she had seen around Saint Maria Goretti Parish, but knew none of them well. She was able to identify them as: Wendy, Mary, Susan, Steve, and Jimmy. Off to the side in the vision were two others: one, who was standing, Gianna recognized as Stefanie. The other who was kneeling, she could not immediately name, but later knew to be Annie.

In the vision Gianna saw Jimmy walk away, then come back. James came in to complete the group of nine. Gianna related the vision to Father Jack Spaulding. In a short time, the seven others in the vision came to Father Spaulding, individually and independently, to tell him about new spiritual experiences that each had recently had. Some thought that they were going crazy because they were hearing voices. Father Spaulding told them about one another.

Father Spaulding told Carol Ameche, a lady of the parish who knows many of the young people, that "It is Our Lady speaking to them, and she has special personal messages for them, for their own growth. And she wants a prayer group to begin in the parish, for young adults, on Friday nights; special things are going to happen in the parish."

Our Lady asked Father Jack and the nine young adults to make a three year commitment to her, not to get married, or enter a seminary, or to make any permanent commitment for three years. At a Thursday evening meeting in early 1991, she said through prophecy, "I will be here with you as long as you honor my Son; consider these three years only the beginning."

Each of the nine young adults, and Father Jack Spaulding also, has been given by Our Lady, through Gianna, a "symbol." This symbol seems to be a virtue or a gift or a fruit of the Holy Spirit that the person is called to grow in, and perhaps that characterizes or should characterize that person. Father Jack's symbol, for instance, is truth. Gianna's symbol is divine love and mercy.

Gianna says this about the symbols, "Our Lady said they were symbols for the world to live by. She did not say we were the example of the symbol for the world to live by. Many people forget we are human and it will take all of our life to achieve the symbol. For example, some people talk about Annie, about how her symbol is humility, and about how she should always reflect humility. But it takes a lifetime to achieve it. It will take my lifetime and only with the grace of God for me to love unconditionally and with His divine mercy." One of the nine young people of Gianna's vision is Annie Ross, the woman we met at the Medjugorje Conference in California.

Chapter 3

Annie

Message from Our Lady, for the parish, May 10, 1990:

*My dear children, please continue to love
and seek my Son in your difficulties. He is
your peace and your strength. Accept your
difficulties with humility and joy. Trust in
my Son. He will give you strength. Accept
yourselves for who you are. I love you my
dear ones, and intercede for you. Pray, pray,
pray! Prayer is the only way to peace in the
world.*

* * *

March 31, 1989. Twenty-five year old Annie Ross was
alone at home. Suddenly someone spoke to her.
Astonished and alarmed, she looked around, searched
the house. She was alone. The voice spoke again, "My
child, I want you to write."

That was the start of a communication between the
Blessed Virgin Mary and Annie which she claims still
continues. Annie, like her parents Dick and Judy Ross,
is outgoing, generous and active. Heavily built, she
looks younger than her age. She is the middle child
and only girl in a family of five. Four years before, in
the summer of 1984, Annie had married a Turkish
Moslem. She gave up her university studies to work
as a realtor, supporting them both while her husband

continued his studies and waited on tables in the evening.

Very soon, Annie realized that those who had advised her against this marriage had been right. The cultural differences and other problems led to the marriage being annulled.

Her spiritual director at that time added to her pain by asking her not to receive Holy Communion because of the process of annulment. Our Lady told her, "Even if something is incorrect, but you obey, I will take care of it." She obeyed for a month and a half, suffering the deprivation of Our Lord, and the public humiliation. Then Father Jack Spaulding asked her what the trouble was. He directed her to return to Holy Communion, which she did with great joy on Easter Sunday 1990.

It all began with Annie when the statue of Our Lady of the Americas was dedicated in the church of Saint Maria Goretti. Father Jack was saying Mass. During the homily Annie heard a voice, a woman's voice speaking to her.

Annie says, "I actually heard a woman's voice outside of me, not inside. I was sitting there in the church full of people, during the homily, and all I was hearing was, 'My child, you must make a decision. You must decide to give your life to me, or not. But you must make the decision now. There is no more time.' So I thought: 'I guess it is time to make this decision.' I walked up to the statue with my flowers, as everyone else was in the church, to place them at her feet. I knelt down and kissed her feet, and I gave her my heart. I told her that she could have any part of me that she wanted; that she could have all of me; that I would make that decision. I walked away sobbing, and went back to my seat. I cried through the rest of the Mass and the rest of the prayers, and it took me about two and a half hours to drive three blocks to my apartment! I arrived home, not realizing that it had taken me so long, and looked at the clock. I thought, 'This is so odd! How could I have possibly taken so long to get home?' I had no idea where I drove, where I was.

"I always left my apartment door open because my brothers, my friends or whoever, would come and go on their way home from work or from friends' houses. They would just pop in and say 'Hi,' or leave me notes or whatever, and I didn't mind them stopping in. It is perfectly safe where I lived.

"I walked in the door and sat down on the couch. I looked at the time, and I was quite puzzled. I heard the same woman's voice say to me, 'My child, I wish for you to write.' I looked around the room, and I said, 'Wait a minute! What's going on?' And I thought, 'You what?' And I heard again, 'My child, I wish for you to write.' I thought perhaps one of my friends was in the room and was making fun of all this, so I went and checked the whole house: every closet, every room, every everything. And there was no one there. About this point I was getting a little frightened, and I thought I had lost my mind. Again I heard the same voice say to me, 'My child I wish for you to write.' It was very gentle, very melodic, very inviting. Not threatening, not anything that would cause me to fear, except for the fact that I was hearing this voice in a room all by myself, and as a human being I was taking all of this and digesting it and saying, 'Wait a minute, this can't be happening.' At the same time I felt an overwhelming peace, joy and serenity.

"Finally I said, 'All right.' And I went to get something to write with. It turned out that the only thing in the house I had to write with was construction paper and crayons. I couldn't find a pen, I couldn't find regular paper, I couldn't find a pencil. I couldn't find anything. I finally found a crayon and a piece of construction paper. One of my friends had been over a little earlier with her small child and we had been coloring. So I started to write. And she began speaking, and her voice was so beautiful. She told me not to be afraid, that she loved me and that I had nothing to fear. She went on speaking, and the crayon wouldn't write, and I was getting very frustrated. Then I finally went and searched for a pencil. I found one. It broke just as I started to write. She had stopped speaking right about this time, and I was searching through the house, until, about ten minutes later I found a pen.

"I began writing all that she had said to me up to that point, word for word, even with punctuation. And I thought 'How interesting that I can remember all of this!' And I sat there; I wrote everything that she had said. As soon as I had finished writing what had been said before the interruption, she began speaking again, and picked up exactly where she had left off in a sentence. I wrote exactly what she was saying. Suddenly she finished speaking; I finished writing, and put everything down. I thought to myself, 'Wow! What just happened to me?' I was filled with incredible peace, and I was so filled with love! I had so much anger, and so much hatred had built up inside of me—because of all of the things I had been through in my life that I was unwilling to let go of—suddenly all of those things were gone. All that hatred and that anger had disappeared. And I was sitting there filled, completely filled with peace. I couldn't believe that I was thinking of people who had hurt me so terribly and wanting to pray for them or wanting to feel sorry for them. It was just so different. I looked up at the clock, but I was very surprised at how long it had taken to write. What seemed to me to be only a few minutes really was quite a long time."

The first Annie actually claimed to see Our Lady was
in a vision connected with a statue of Our Lady of
Guadalupe. She had seen the statue (about two and a
half feet high) in a shop, and felt strongly urged to buy
it. She told her mother who bought it for her. Annie
took it home and set it up in her bedroom. Immediately the room was filled with the perfume of roses.
She says, "I screamed for the others, and they came
right down and said, 'Wow!' It was so profuse and so
strong."

Then on December 11, 1989, Annie was in bed, sick.
She had asked her guardian angel to wake her so that
she could pray the Rosary at the same time as the people in church. Suddenly a brilliant light lit up the
room and Annie says Our Lady spoke, saying to her:
"Look at me; really look at me." As Annie describes
it: "Out of the statue I saw a form just in the same
shape as the statue, but of many different intensities
of light. The dress was twinkling with stars, brilliant
stars." Annie looked from the statue to a picture of
the Sacred Heart of Jesus, next to it. She saw, superim-
posed on the picture, the face of Mary. Annie says that
the whole room was illumined with scintillating stars
and changing lights of pinks, purples and blues.

Annie says that both Our Lord and Our Lady spoke
to her. She says their voices are real voices, sometimes
exterior, sometimes interior. Our Lord's voice is majes-
tic. He does not appear to her, but she has seen Him
in visions. He is beautiful beyond description.

Eventually Annie found courage to take the written
messages to Father Jack. At first she just sent them
to him without comment, but he did not respond,
though she saw him each day at Mass. So she went
along, as she says, realizing that she must be committed to the Lord, but nonetheless sobbing, afraid that:
"I would have to be a nun." Father Jack received her

lovingly, prayed with her and commented on the beauty of the messages. Annie says, "Father Jack knew me very well; knew the mistakes I had made and the things I had often argued about with him at my family's dinner table." But he knew too that she was now at daily Mass and was trying to change. All he asked was that she be humble.

Annie's symbol is humility. At that time, she says, she was probably one of the most arrogant people around. Our Lady has warned her of the suffering that will come from the unbelief of others. She has learned from Our Lady that to be humble is to serve the Father unconditionally, with total love. It is to give to others unceasingly, with love. A special task given to Annie is to pray for priests and religious.

Like the other eight, Annie was asked for a commitment. Hers began later than the others, on April 1, 1989, and was for two years.

On December 21, 1989, while Annie was at the Thursday evening prayer group, she felt herself pulled to her knees. She states Our Lady spoke to her, saying that she would appear to her on the 28th, and that she was to fast meanwhile. The following Thursday, December 28, during the Rosary in the church of Saint Maria Goretti, Our Lady appeared to Annie. A brilliant light of green, orange and yellow surrounded the statue. Mary seemed to step out from it and to take flesh. She does not look like the statue, though often her dress remains the same. This was the same day and time that the Blessed Virgin appeared to Gianna. Annie says they were kneeling in different benches. Gianna and Annie share these Thursday apparitions, but Annie says, Our Lady speaks to them separately. Sometimes they see her differently. She comes as *Mother of Mercy* and as *Our Lady of Joy.*

Unexpectedly, in October 1990 the Blessed Mother

told Annie that she would no longer appear to her regularly. But for the remaining years of her life she will come on her birthday, and additionally, at other times, especially in times of difficulty and need. The difficulty may be a trial in Annie's life, or, she says, it may be some need of which the Blessed Mother knows. So Annie no longer sees Our Lady often, not even every Thursday, but she constantly sees her as a form of light, just as she did before the actual apparitions. But sometimes she does see her on Thursday nights when she kneels with Gianna saying the Rosary, and also at other times.

"During that apparition" [when Our Lady told Annie that the time of frequent apparitions was over], says Annie, "she was so beautiful! She was more beautiful and more radiant than I had ever seen her. I couldn't even tell you how beautiful she was. . .She thanked me (thanking *me*!) for giving my life to her. . . . I cried when she left. I wasn't crying because she was gone, but because I had not done enough. Even if I were to give every moment for the rest of my life for her, it will never be enough."

CHAPTER 4

Steve and Wendy

Message from Our Lady for the parish, September 6, 1990:

My dear children, please focus all your attention on my Son. You spend far too much energy worrying about what is to come and preparing for that time. My dear, dear children, please pray for peace. Pray, pray, pray! Focus all your attention on my Son, and place all your energy in Him. I am your comforting mother, your loving one who listens and loves you. Pray. Please pray. Thank you my dear ones for responding to my call.

* * *

Steve and Wendy Nelson are brother and sister. They both are blonde and handsome. They have an accent different from that of the other seven young adults; they grew up in South Dakota and Nebraska. There is something in both their personalites of the great plains and open spaces of the beginning of the American West. The Nelson family lives behind Saint Maria Goretti's church and has five members: Steve and Wendy, their parents, and their fifteen year old sister Jenny. Their father works for Giant Oil Industries.

The younger of the two, Wendy was born on the feast of the Assumption of the Blessed Virgin Mary, August

15, 1969. She is blonde, very good looking, informal, straightforward. She speaks not at all in abstractions, but concretely.

In 1987 Wendy went to live with the Missionaries of Charity, the religious congregation of Mother Teresa of Calcutta, in Phoenix. She stayed there, living with them, not as a postulant or novice, but simply as a lay person sharing the life of the sisters. It was they who taught Wendy to pray continually. "They are my friends," she says. After a year and a half she moved back to live with her family.

She still works daily with the sisters; she works with children, children of all kinds, white, black, hispanic, from what are called "the projects," housing for poorer people. When we first met her, she had just come from the last day of a bible camp that Mother Teresa's sisters run for two or three weeks every summer for children from "the projects." "It's been a gift for me, spiritually, learning from the sisters, and then trying to teach it to the kids." When asked if we could take her picture, she said, "Sure, but I look pretty bad, I've had sixty or seventy kids from South Phoenix hanging on me all day."

In 1987, Wendy became dissatisfied with her life as a student and a member of a sorority at Arizona State University. She quit school, came home to Scottsdale, began to go to prayer groups, began to go to Mass during the week, eventually began to go to Mass every day and to talk to Father Jack Spaulding often.

One day, at home, she heard someone say, "Will you give me everything?" She thought, "What's going on here?" Then she heard the same voice and the same words again, and she said to herself, "This is Jesus talking!" Wendy says, "Then I went to Father Jack and I told him what happened; Gianna had already been to see him, and Stefanie, and a couple of others. Father

Jack said to just keep it real quiet, to come often and we'll talk about it. Then, every now and then I'd be praying and They'd just say something. Maybe something about Jesus' agony and His passion. Gianna was getting messages. Then Father Jack called us all together and said, "Look, you all are having these things happen." And that's how I got involved in it.

"The first time we all got together was in August [1988]. That summer things had begun to happen, and then towards the end of the summer we all kind of figured out that everything was happening to all of us. And Father Jack put the pieces together for us."

Asked if she had seen the Blessed Virgin Mary, Wendy said, "One time, on a Thursday night, it must have been after the Rosary, I saw her, she's **beautiful!** It was really neat, because two nights before that I kept seeing this light around her statue, all around her statue, this really bright light. It got so bright that it was just hurting my eyes; so I closed my eyes. And finally Our Lady says, 'Child, look at me.' And I could not, I just couldn't look. And then she says, 'Child, look at me with the innocence and purity of a child.' Then she just came out of the statue. It was beautiful, one of the most beautiful things!"

Asked, "Did she speak to you then?" Wendy answered, "No, we didn't talk; she was just there. It's the kind of thing you never forget, it's always in the heart; and it's funny, when I talk about it I can just feel it! Oh! the love that comes from her! It's just **incredible!** I'd never experienced love in that way. It was a great experience. Beautiful gifts from Them." [Authors' note: Father Jack and the nine young adults often refer to "Them"; this means Jesus and Mary.]

In the summer of 1991 there was a desecration of the Blessed Sacrament at Saint Maria Goretti church. Wendy, going into the chapel to pray at five in the morning, found the Hosts scattered everywhere. This deeply upset her.

Besides her daily prayer before the Real Presence, Wendy is at Mass each day. Often she reads the *divine office*. Her great devotion is to Jesus in His sufferings. Books which talk about Jesus and His suffering are her main spiritual reading.

Jesus and Mary speak to her frequently in words that are real and definite. "They talk to me," Wendy says, "teaching me faith, trust. They come like a friend. They talk back to me. Sometimes they speak every day. Sometimes I'll go a week without hearing anything. They bring me a lot of peace. It's been like that since that first time when they asked me, 'Would you give me everything?' The other day when I was praying with many distractions [Wendy's health was in a worrying state], Our Lady said, 'Please pray with your heart. Trust. Pray.' That way the problems of my mind would be relieved."

As for marriage or joining a religious order, Wendy is open, "I leave it to divine inspiration. At that moment, they'll let me know, and I'll do it. They decide."

Wendy's symbol is strength. "I myself don't see myself as strong, I know what my weakness is," Wendy said.

She will return to the Arizona State University as a second semester sophomore, to major probably in sociology. She feels now that she is stronger, and could give Christian witness, even to some of the people who knew her before. She adds, "If that's what God has in mind."

About the other eight young people, Wendy says, "There's a sort of bonding among us; I couldn't have made it without God working through them, without their support and their love. Too many times I've gotten too involved down in South Phoenix. In a sense we [the nine young adults] are a community. I need them. We all have a bonding." And she says, "Father Jack has told us that whether here, now, or in the future, we're all going to see her [Our Lady]." And this is the basis of the bond among them.

When we met Wendy and Steve in the summer of 1990, they were off to Anaheim's Disneyland, "My favorite place," says Wendy!

Wendy's older brother, Steve, is in his mid-twenties, five feet nine inches tall; he has long blonde hair, big shoulders and chest. He is heavy but with no fat, an athlete. With a wonderful outgoing personality, he speaks articulately without using big words.

About his sister Steve says, "Wendy and I have always been close because of the way we grew up. We grew up in ranch country where our closest neighbor was twenty miles away. So she was my play partner and I was hers. The Nebraska-South Dakota line crossed right through our place. Then we spent a long time in North Platte, Nebraska. So Wendy and I basically grew up together."

Steve has an Associate of Arts degree from the local community college. He studied for an agricultural degree in livestock management at the University of Stevenville, Texas; he had gone there on a rodeo scholarship. He switched to a general business major when he came back to Scottsdale and enrolled in the community college.

Steve has begun a course at Stevenville Community College studying for a diploma as a Medical Technician. He hopes to get a job with an ambulance company, and eventually to become a fireman. His first and dearest ambition had been to be champion steer wrestler and roper. At least temporarily he has given up competing in rodeos because he felt that Jesus and

Mary asked that of him. At first he said to himself that, at least, they could not possibly ask him to give up his calf wrestling and roping. He would hold on to that! Then, feeling that he must give everything, he put the whole of his life "on hold." He went into the church of Saint Maria Goretti and, kneeling before the tabernacle, he told the Lord, "I've done it." No answer. He repeated, "I've done it." No answer. He repeated, "I've done it!" Silence. "Did you hear what I said?" he asked. Steve laughs, remembering how he expected bells to ring and heavenly rejoicing to break out.

He has established a habit of daily Mass, of fasting and Eucharistic adoration. He talks to Jesus telling Him how he feels, and Jesus responds in his heart. He draws courage and strength from the Lord. Sometimes it is Mary whom he feels speaking in his heart. Still, as Steve says, "I walk by faith."

Like the others, Steve has a symbol given to him by Mary. His symbol is faith. Wendy says that Steve is like Peter in the gospels; and he is in many ways. His birthday is August 6, the Feast of the Transfiguration, an event in which the apostle Peter figured strongly.

Asked if he felt called to become a priest, Steve answered, "When all this started, that's the first thing that came to my mind, 'My gosh! I'm going to have to be a priest,' and I went through the whole ordeal of: 'Wait a minute, being a priest isn't so bad,' actually to the point where I accepted it, except for the fact that I couldn't. It just didn't set right. It was my mom that said to me one morning, 'What's marriage? Chopped liver?' " Marriage is what Steve would like. He has been dating a beautiful girl for three years. Another talent he has is singing country music. He has been encouraged to take this up with a band. Steve says, "I don't know what will happen next year. I don't know what will happen next month. All I know is I feel I

am doing what I'm supposed to be doing right now.
And however They work it out, that's the way it will
go.

"My ultimate goal in life I guess, since I was real
little, has been to be world champion calf roper and
steer wrestler on the rodeos. It's the way I grew up.
I've ridden horses since I was very little. That was one
thing that I put on hold for right now. I don't know
what will happen with that, I don't know. It is hard
to put into words something that I know I need to do.
I would love to do it. It's up to Them though, up to
Jesus and Mary. Because that's basically who I am
now. I'm totally at Their disposal. That's who I am. If
They decide they would like me to represent Them in
that form, then that's what I'll do. But I don't know
if I'm to be a priest, or if I'm to rope; I don't know."

We asked Steve how he became involved in what is
happening to him and to the other eight young people
of the parish. He said that about four years ago, "I was
still going to church to keep mom and dad happy, but
I lived in Gilbert which is twenty-four miles from here
even though it is still city. And I wasn't living the kind
of life I should have been living. I was working hard
and going out on Friday and Saturday nights.

"I don't know why I started coming up here more,
and next thing I know I couldn't get enough of it. I
started becoming more involved up here, and we got a
Young Adult Group going. Eventually I moved back up
here. I guess that was when They made the real conversion step in my life. I started praying and going to daily
Mass. I didn't know why. If you had told me that a year
before I started, I would have told you you were crazy.
I didn't have anything against church. I guess it was
just the rebellious side I was going through."

The Young Adult group grew, and Steve gradually
became one of the leaders in the group. "Then on Sep-

tember 18, 1988, Father Jack talked to me in his office.
I had talked to him a bunch before. He was my
spiritual guide and confessor through my whole conversion. He told me that Our Lady had something very
special planned, and that she would like to use me. He
said it was totally an invitation.

"You know, your first reaction is to kind of want to
disbelieve. You are overwhelmed. It has grown from
there. I know it has never been pushed on me, and I
have never been able to push myself at it. I have had to
realize that anything that is going to happen is going to
happen in Their time. They are going to take it the way
They want to take it. Of course in the beginning I had
dreams of grandeur and illusions of all different things
that They would be doing, and nothing happened the
way I thought it would. But now as I am going along
I see more and more that there has been a lot that's happened. And most of it I didn't even see happening, I was
so busy in my head with what was supposed to happen.
I think I've changed a lot. It comes down to this: I'm no
better and no worse than anybody else.

"It was last Easter that I realized that there was only
one difference between Peter and Judas. They both
denied Our Lord, both the same. Peter knew of, and
pleaded for, God's mercy. Judas didn't think he could
be forgiven. And that's the difference between the two.
I guess that's why I know I can be forgiven. I know
I'm going to sin again, even though I thought, 'Wow,
get into this and I'm just going to be this pure and perfect person.'

"I think it is my sinfulness that makes me more real
in helping people. I still have just as many stumbling
stones as the next person. And I also see that in order
to truly be an example I've got to stop worrying about
tomorrow. And I can't dwell on yesterday.

"Like Peter stepping out of the boat. . .I'm taking

each step knowing that there is going to be something under my feet to catch me. I feel if I can do that, that will be the greatest witness I can give for God, because right now I'm going through struggles just like a lot of the people I talk to.

"Our Lord and Our Lady can't want me to be anything more than what I am. They called me as Steve Nelson, the way Steve Nelson was, because they loved who I am. And I think if I was to be some special person, like those people who want to make me that—that come here or that have been here before—I think it would defeat the whole purpose of Our Lady using me. God has got every power in the world to do this.

"For example: if He wanted to appear to me right now, He could wave His hand over me and say, 'You're never going to sin any more; you're going to be perfect.' I'm going to be unattainable to anyone else here. No one is going to want to listen to me.

"They're going to say, 'Yes, isn't this just great. This prayer stuff is really neat. It's really good for you, but you don't have to work, you don't sin any more. But look at me. I have to get up every morning, I've got to put a roof over my head. I've got a wife; or I'm thinking about getting married. Maybe I'm still having trouble with this sin that I've got that I just can't get rid of. I go in and I confess and I do it again next week.'

"If they took me as more than what I am, what good would I be for Them? I think that's where my greatest example is, I'm just me.

"I don't know what I'll be in the future, but I do know that as I stand right now today, I believe with all of my heart that there is a God and God is great. And I know that if I truly trust and truly believe, it may not always work out the way I want it to, but everything will be taken care of.

"And I know that some people, it would shake them

up, other people it would make them feel better that I don't have a direct plug-in to God. But I think overall, it's just my humanness that They want to use. Gosh, if God didn't want to use humans He could just come down right now and say, 'This is it!'

"It's something we are all called to: to be an example with our lives. To the best of my knowledge, and all the things I've learned up to now, I could say that this sometimes embarrasses me that any of this goes on. It's stuff we should have been doing a long time ago. Now everybody makes out that it's so great. Probably in God's eyes it's a bare minimum. I don't think we can do enough ever to thank Him or to trust Him and believe in Him. I still find myself looking down at the water and sinking a little bit sometimes. I probably always will.

"If there's any way I can express myself, it is just that I am who I am, and hopefully that will be enough to do what They want to do. I can't change it; I tried. When it all first started I thought: 'Here I am, and They want to use me. I'm going to be something great. I'm going to have all the answers to everything. Money won't be a problem. I won't be rich, but everything will be taken care of. I won't have those worries. I'm just going to work on Our Lady's plan. Everything will be fine.' The one thing she has shown me is: 'Steve, working on my plan is that I need you to be you, and to show people that even though you have hard times, even though things go up and down, if you have hope and trust you can still carry around that joy and that peace that I know.'

"Susan Evans is a good friend. She's a beautiful girl. Now that's a girl! She's going through pain no one can imagine. Still, with the attitude she's got—in my eyes she's really something. She was kind of the catalyst for me.

"Susan met my mom, and my mom told Susan about me. Then my mom coaxed me up to church one evening and said, 'There's a girl who wants to talk to you.' I was kind of hesitant, and I tried to get away, but Susan met me at the front door of the church and sat and talked to me. She gave me that extra push to do what I was feeling in my heart I needed to do. She is the one who started the Young Adult group that we've got going really strong now. She has been a kind of catalyst for all of us."

Steve

Wendy

CHAPTER 5

Susan

Message from Our Lady for the parish, November 1, 1990:

My dear children, come to my Son in all of your imperfections and weaknesses, in openness. Do not hide from my Son. He is your Friend, Spouse and Brother. He truly loves you and will guide you if you allow Him. Oh my dear children, how my Son loves you! You do not have control over your desires. You are powerless before our God. Open your hearts to Him, and know the truth. Be fruitful servants by following the Word of God. I bless you my dear ones, and my Son blesses you. Thank you for your response to my call. Peace be to you.

* * *

"The most important thing is that Our Lady is calling us to return to God." So Susan Evans sums up the intervention of the Mother of God in our times. "That is what the messages are all about; wherever she is appearing or speaking, it is a call to return to God."

Susan's role in the Scottsdale events seems to be mainly one of suffering. All the nine suffer in one way or another, so that Gianna was moved to say, "I

50

wouldn't wish for anyone to see the Blessed Virgin, because so much suffering results."

Dark-haired Susan is an attractive lady, personable and straightforward, a strong character. In 1987, when she was twenty-nine, she was a guest at a wedding reception. Sitting with her family at a table in the garden, she was startled to hear a voice asking, "Would you give up your family for Me?" She says, "We were at a round table; I looked at each one of them, and I finally answered, 'Yes Lord, because I love you the more.' Then, all of a sudden, I saw the miracle of the sun [the sun spinning, a phenomenon frequently seen at Medjugorje]. I thought, 'I didn't see that!' Then the whole sky turned rose, and I thought, 'No, I didn't see that!' I had answered the question because I knew where it was coming from, but to *see* something visible! My first thought was, 'No, no, no.' That night, the sun came down and the moon went up and it looked like it was on fire, and I said: 'I did see that!'

"The next thing Our Lord asked of me was: 'Would you suffer for Me?' Of all places, I was at the State Fair. Of all places to pick! There were a lot of people around. The next thing He showed me was: 'Would you suffer for this person?'—He picked out a particular person. The guy had long hair, a beard, dirty jeans. He looked like someone one would think was the lowest of the people. I said, 'Yes.' Then He picked out a woman. She could have been American Indian or Spanish. She was a real heavy woman. She could have been someone I might have looked down on. He asked me: 'Would you suffer for her?' I said, 'Yes.' Later on He showed me that: 'Your "yes" is because I gave you the grace to say "yes"; not because of anything you did.'"

In 1987 Susan had heard a voice saying to her, "Pray to the Blessed Mother." "Initially," Susan says, "I was afraid of her because she is so pure and holy—and here

I am! I was scared of her. But I started praying to her with all my heart. And the change! I wasn't even going to church at that time. All I ever asked of her was to bring me back to Our Lord; to bring me back to church. I prayed and prayed and prayed.

"Within five or six weeks I was back in church. I showed up at Saint Maria Goretti church at five o'clock. Then I heard: 'Go to confession to Father Jack.' It was the last thing I would have said to myself! I went to Mass there the next day. My mom was there. She said, 'What are you here for?' I looked at her! I said 'Oh I don't know. I've come to keep you company.' I started going to Mass every day, and I started staying after Mass for a couple of hours to pray. Then I would come back two hours later. I would go to Mass twice a day—I was so drawn to the Eucharist. I cried receiving the Eucharist, because it is such a gift, and because Our Lord had brought me away from a sinful life to a better life."

Suffering was not long in coming. Physical suffering. Susan developed lupus, fibro myalgia, and scleroderma. Of the pain, she says, "I know that even if a person is physically suffering, if someone treats them with kindness and love, it makes up for the physical pain. If you dwell on your suffering, which is easy to do, you are going to hurt more. But to pray and be filled with His peace, His love, His joy, then your suffering is easier." But she observes that when doctors have difficulty in diagnosing symptoms, they think the causes must be psychological. So the suffering is intensified. On one occasion, after having had a particularly difficult time from a doctor, she read somewhere that many doctors can no longer heal, because of their lack of love of God. The Lord she says, is her physician.

Spiritual suffering followed. Our Lord had warned

Susan to expect a struggle. "I said, 'OK, I'm going to make it a good one.'"

When Susan was a child she many times dreamed of chastisements that were to come on the world. She was never frightened by these dreams. But in September 1988 Our Lord began to speak to her about these chastisements. She found herself agonizing in extreme fear, not for herself but for those who do not believe; and for those who, believing, do not return to God. She struggled with this and other temptations for many weeks.

"I started really good for two and a half months," she says. Then, "Finally I got mad at God! And I told Him so, and afterwards He just filled me with peace. I had been hiding my feelings inside myself. You can't hide anything from Him anyway, but because I just expressed it to Him and let it out, He just filled me with so much peace. It really gives the devil nothing to work with once you have let it out to God." Susan adds, "I learned so much through all this. I really thanked Our Lord afterwards."

During this time Susan moved into an apartment of her own. She gave away all she possessed, taking with her only her dog Joshua. As she has considerable hearing loss, he alerts her to the door bell. These days possessions are starting to accumulate again, but that does not worry Susan. Having once given away her treasures, the detachment remains and she says she could dispose of everything in a second if Jesus asked it of her.

Both Jesus and Mary have spoken audibly to Susan, though not often, but she converses with them all day in an interior, normal way. She does not see either of Them, but says that once when the tabernacle was opened, she saw the face of Jesus, crowned with thorns. One of the occasions on which Susan heard Our Lady was when the Blessed Mother told her, in November 1987, that she wished to start a prayer group of young adults, and that she would herself guide it. When Susan replied that she was too sick, Mary responded, *Trust me.* Six months later, when she was even worse, Our Lady reiterated, *Trust me.*

In these days Susan suffers physical pain, emotional pain, spiritual pain, which Jesus asks her to share. But she says, she would rather talk about the Lord than about herself. She knows what suffering He has for her in the future, but she takes one day at a time, not knowing day by day what He wants.

When she becomes very ill she is unable to leave the house and depends on Holy Communion being brought to her. During her trials, which she thinks of as failures, Susan says she learned understanding. Before, when, for example she was asked to visit a man who was dying of cancer, and she heard him "yelling and screaming at everyone," she could not understand a person being like that until she herself yelled at the Lord. After her own suffering and her failure to cope with it, she observed, "I told Our Lord the other day, 'You know, a righteous person can't really lead a person back to You. It is a sinner who leads a sinner back to You, because a sinner has understanding. A righteous person will sit down and say, 'What did you do that for?' A sinner would say, 'I understand.' I can be kinder to someone who is bad because I saw myself there."

Susan's symbol is charity. To her it means as she says, "Giving of yourself. It is a giving of the gifts you have received: love, faith, hope, joy. It is a giving of those gifts to others. At one time I was afraid of this symbol, because charity is also a giving of yourself to Our Lord. It got a little scary there for a while because He was asking me to suffer."

"All I know about," she says, "is how to bring someone to the Lord. That is what Our Lord and Our Blessed

Mother have taught me. I know that Our Lady is the one who really brought me to the Lord. That is all I prayed for. I didn't want anything else; I just wanted Our Lord; I wanted to come back to church. I wanted God. That is why we hear, 'Seek first the kingdom of God, and all else will be given to you.' Inner strength will be given to you; you will be filled with joy, peace, happiness."

Meanwhile Susan, confined to her house, prays as much as she can. She says that Our Lord has taught her that we cannot pray enough. Even twenty-four hours is not enough.

Events at Scottsdale have not been a surprise to Susan. When she was a child she often dreamed about Our Lord coming from Heaven with arms outstretched. When she heard of Medjugorje she believed instantly, but because of something she knew, she said to Our Lady, "But I thought you meant you would come here?"

She sums up her relationship with Our Lord: "I tell him everyday that I love Him. I think He likes that. Even if I am not feeling very well, I tell Him, 'I feel terrible, real lousy, but I love You anyway!' And if I make a mistake, or I fail, I say, 'I love You anyway. You created me like this!'" Our Lord likes humor!"

CHAPTER 6

James, Mary, and Jimmy

Message from Our Lady to the Parish, July 12, 1990:

> *My dear children, there is hope in my Son.*
> *Please be strong. If you are not strong now*
> *and endure what my Son sends you, you will*
> *not be able to endure what is to come. Have*
> *hope, and place all your trust and confidence*
> *in my Son. Pray my children. Pray. Thank*
> *you for responding to my call.*

* * *

James Pauley, six foot two, is in his early twenties, the youngest of the nine young adults of Gianna's vision. He is reserved but friendly, warm and gentle. He lives at home with his parents and two brothers, one younger and one older. He is planning to move in with two friends.

James had not yet seen Our Lady nor received any messages or interior locutions when we spoke with him in the fall of 1991. Before any of these events began, James had visited Medjugorje in 1987. That alone was as he says, "the beginning of a lot of wonderful things." He became part of the Scottsdale events because he was one of those in Gianna's vision of the nine seeing Our Lady.

In 1988 Father Jack Spaulding told him that he was "one of Mary's children." James says, "I don't know exactly what that means." At first James said it was hectic and he was excited at the thought of seeing Our Lady. It took him a while to cool and be disciplined. Now he lives day by day because he says, "Our Lord is not in the past or the future, but here now."

Like the other eight young people, he tries to go to Mass daily, and spends time in personal prayer. A good experience for him was when he went off alone to the New Mexico Monastery of Christ in the Desert for five days of prayer. Another project was a journey to Mexico with Wendy to work with the poor. Among other things there, he helped to build a house for a poor family. Putting a roof over their heads really appealed to James, and he would like eventually to find a ministry among the poor. His symbol is courage.

James works full time for the parish of Saint Maria Goretti. At first he was Youth Minister and director of the Teen Program for high school students in the parish, leading the Teen prayer group of sixty or seventy teenagers. The group says the "Scriptural Rosary," share spontaneous prayer, and then at the end they pray over those with special needs. Since July, 1991, he works with the Confirmation program for sixteen year olds. This is a three year program leading up to the Sacrament.

He has considerable responsibility for the young adult prayer group that meets on Friday nights. James also organizes their twice yearly three day camping retreat which draws fifty or so young adults. In late spring of 1991, James made a speaking tour of England and Wales together with Father Jack Spaulding. The contacts he made there with young people in Britain are bearing fruit in a link-up of young adults' prayer groups. James likes what he does; "I've grown a lot, working; I've matured a lot," he says.

James attends Scottsdale Community College full time, being in his third year. He will go on in 1992 to Arizona State University, or perhaps to a seminary. Athletic, he plays basketball in the city recreation league. So, with full time work, he has a heavy schedule.

Among the nine young adults, James is perhaps closest to Mary Cook and Jimmy Kupanoff.

*   *   *

Mary Cook, in her late twenties, attractive, quietly radiant, yet down to earth, has as her symbol: hope. We first met her at the Good Egg restaurant where she was working at the time as a waitress. She was, in fact, an outstanding waitress, obviously underemployed. She had attended Arizona State University for one year, and then stopped.

When we saw Mary in early 1991, she no longer worked at the restaurant. She had for a while helped with the Teen program of the parish, with James Pauley. In particular, Mary met with the teenagers regularly at their Sunday meeting. About sixty-five were coming at that time. The Sunday meeting, complementary to the teenagers' Monday night prayer group, is more of a teaching session.

Then she had the opportunity to begin a work which is dear to her heart—"The Precious Ones Pre-School," where she has about fifteen or twenty children, most of whom stay all day. Mary works in cooperation with her highly qualified staff and with the parents to provide a Christian foundation for these children.

Mary Cook has a strong gift of discernment in prayer, to distinguish what comes from the Lord from what does not come from Him, especially to know how He wants to lead her, what He calls her to do. "In my life, I just have to discern, to pray hard, to know what He wants me to do; now I have confidence in what I learn from spiritual direction and from my prayer. Whatever it is, I've got to pray about it." Jesus and Mary speak to her: "She just talks to me," Mary says, "always. And if I talk to Him, He just talks right to me."

But when she began receiving messages during the Young Adults Friday prayer meeting, Mary cringed, doubted, and even ran away. Up to the fall of 1991, Our Lady has apparently appeared twice to Mary, but always she sees a glow of purple light round the statue of Mary in the church. "My eyes hurt when I'm looking at her," Mary says, "and during the Joyful Mysteries of the Rosary on Thursday, she speaks to me." Mary hears clearly the message given to Gianna during the Thursday prayer.

Like Stefanie, Steve, Gianna, James, Steve and Annie, Mary is a Eucharistic minister in the parish of Saint Maria Goretti. She goes to daily Mass and spends time before the Blessed Sacrament, especially in the evening. During the day, she talks frequently with Jesus and with Mary.

* * *

Jimmy Kupanoff went with his family to Medjugorje in 1987, before the Scottsdale events began. There he had a strong realization of Jesus as Lord of everything. He began to pray. A deeper conversion resulted. He started to notice the "small miracles" in life.

When his family moved back to Ohio, Jimmy felt he should return to Scottsdale. For a while he lived at the rectory with Father Jack and Father Eric. Then his family too returned. Jimmy, born in May 1968, is the oldest of six: three sisters and two young brothers. He studies as a junior at Arizona State University and will major in communications. He also works part time, delivering magazines for real estate companies. In the summer of 1991, Jimmy spent six weeks in Mexico improving his Spanish, which is fluent.

He does not yet see the Blessed Virgin, though she has spoken to him a few times, in clear words, in his heart. Otherwise he receives messages from her mostly through Gianna.

Jimmy's symbol is compassion.

Jimmy   *Mary*

CHAPTER 7

Stefanie

(Extract from a message to the Young Adults' Prayer Group, given by Jesus, through Gianna, September 6, 1991):

I am your Jesus Who loves you. I am here with you to tell you of My love and to shed My graces upon you. Know, My dear ones, that as you suffer, your suffering is redemptive and for a purpose, all which you will all see with time, in the light. Oh, how I love you and call you to be My dear beloved disciples. Be childlike. Be filled with my joy. Be carefree. Do not be somber. Your struggles and self contempt will only bring glory to the reign of God. I bless each and every one of you.

. . . In silence I go around this room. Receive the gift of My Spirit, Who heals silently, quietly, in the whisper of the wind. A rebirth for you. Listen. Open your hearts. I want to embrace you. Give to Me now your fear, your doubt, your questions. Receive My answer, My trust, My peace, My joy, My dignity, My respect, My courage, My compassion, My love, and My divine mercy. Receive now, as I bless each and every one of you with special graces this night. Be open, and in silence, as I walk this room now.

> *Now I pray for you to My Father. Oh, dear*
> *Abba, My Daddy, I present to you My dear*
> *beloved disciples, who stand by Me, who walk*
> *with Me, who love in Me and give you glory.*
> *Place your protection and seal of love. They*
> *are My army. They are Mine. They are yours.*
> *They are Ours in the Trinity. Amen. Amen.*
> *Amen.*

*   *   *

The young adults' prayer group meets every Friday
night from 7:30 until about 9:00. Anyone from eighteen years old to thirty-five is welcome. Father Jack
Spaulding and Carol Ameche lead the meeting. During
the school year, about fifty young people attend. They
sit in a circle around the Blessed Sacrament in the new
chapel, called the "Tabernacle."

The group says the five Sorrowful Mysteries of the
Rosary, and then the Chaplet of Divine Mercy, both
very slowly. There follows a time for prayers of peti-
tion, during which all hold hands. Usually in the time
for petitions, Jesus or Mary gives a message.

Three of the nine young people attend the young
adults' prayer group regularly on Friday evenings,
Stefanie Staab, Mary Cook, James Pauley; sometimes,
Gianna Talone and Annie Ross attend. It seems Jesus
speaks through Gianna, Our Lady and sometimes
Jesus, speak through Stefanie, and occasionally
through Annie. Recently Mary Cook has been receiving
messages for the group, both from Jesus and from
Mary. All these messages are for the prayer group, and
many take the form of prophecies. The prophecies seem
unusually strong, much stronger than those found, for
example, in an ordinary and perhaps charismatic
prayer group. There have been other prophecies, from
other persons, during the prayer meeting, but these

have almost always been confirmed as un-authentic by Jesus and Mary speaking to Gianna and to Stefanie.

The prophecies in the young adults' prayer group are often in a teaching mode, presenting some aspect or part of basic Christian doctrine. In the earliest days of the young people's group, they met in the sacristy of the church. Maybe because the number was small, Jesus and Mary responded directly to the requests and questions of individual persons, speaking through Stefanie and Gianna. Carol Ameche, who along with Father Jack Spaulding is one of the two older persons usually present in the prayer group, asked for a more generous heart. Jesus responded that she already had a generous heart, and should ask for the grace of abandonment. Our Lady, in response to a prayer for aborted babies, told the group one night through Stefanie, that "people need to know that aborted babies go directly to her care, and they are with her, for they are innocent victims of the sin; and that penitent and reconciled mothers need to know that their babies are praying for them."

As well as at the Friday night young adult meetings, Mary often speaks through Stefanie and Gianna to individual persons at the Thursday night meetings in the Church. Until recently, people were invited to come forward after Mass for individual prayers for healing, to be prayed over by Father Spaulding and members of the group present. Many spiritual, emotional and physical healings occurred.

Stefanie Staab is a beautiful young woman, tall and personable, gracious, intelligent. Stefanie graduated with a B.S. degree from Arizona State University, and at present works as a bank accountant. In the fall of 1990, Father Faricy went to Dallas to see her; she had

gone there for three months to work for a financial
firm as a consultant regarding a mortage portfolio.

Stefanie was born September 9, 1962. Her parents
divorced when Stefanie was five years old; both remar-
ried and have since been divorced again. When asked
how come she turned out as well as she did with such
a difficult family background, she answered, "I didn't
'turn out' like this; Mary came, and she did a lot for
me." She adds, "I've softened up a lot; I'm more like
who I think God created me to be." Stefanie says that
her life has turned around since the Blessed Virgin
Mary began to come to Saint Maria Goretti Parish, and
that her family is quite happy about that. At the present time she lives with her mother in the parish. Stefanie's father lives in New York. Stefanie has an older
sister, married, Laurie Spinelli, and a younger brother,
Craig, also married.

One of Stefanie's hobbies is skiing. She and Craig
share an enthusiasm for target shooting. Stefanie
listens to Christian music and jazz: "I like jazz a lot,"
she says with enthusiasm. She listens to Christian
music when she jogs (four times a week), especially
Sandi Patti and a group called "A Capella." "They do
all acapella singing, no instruments, and they have my
favorite song, 'Criminal on the Clouds,' about the good
thief crucified with Jesus. It's just like praying," she
says, "and it really picks me up."

Since August of 1988 Stefanie has received messages
from Our Lady not only during the young adults'
prayer meetings, but daily messages up until the fall
of 1989. Since then, she has received messages outside
the prayer group less frequently. The messages are
almost always teachings, usually fairly long. She has
not seen Our Lady, only spoken with her, and she
speaks with her frequently. Stefanie writes down the
private messages and gives them to Father Spaulding.

They contain "a lot of instruction, just like from a mother. She's told me the good things about myself and the bad things about myself, the things that I should change." Stefanie does not expect to see the Blessed Mother. This is the significance of her being seen standing in Gianna's vision of the group of nine. Gianna has been told that whereas people will come to her seeking the divine love and mercy of Jesus, Stefanie's part will be to write and to be sent out to speak.

During the prayer group Stefanie is more like a mouthpiece. Jesus also speaks to her, teaches her about Himself, about His heart, about the arrogance of the world, about conversion, and that we will be punished. "I feel like a lady-in-waiting sometimes, kind of waiting for Him to tell me what to do—the next thing."

When asked about the relationships among the nine young adults, Stefaine said that they are close. She has been a roommate of Mary Cook and of Annie. Gianna is "like an older sister." Stefanie worked for Annie's father for a while, as a consultant. She is a good friend of Susan Evans in particular, very aware of Susan's suffering.

When the Blessed Virgin Mary gave a "symbol" to each of the nine persons that Gianna saw in her vision, as well as to Father Jack Spaulding, the symbol she gave to Stefanie is "joy." In fact, Stefanie is joyful, she laughs easily, she radiates a kind of gladness.

* * *

Extract from a message to the Young Adults' Prayer Group, given by Jesus, through Stefanie, January 26, 1990:

My dear ones, how I long for your intimacy.
I see the deepest incentives of your heart. I

your thoughts, your joy, your sorrow, your
fear, your struggles, your happiness, all the
moments of your day with Me.*

*Do not come to hear My words, come to live
My words and be the truth, My example for
the salvation of souls. It is your actions that
speak truth. . .There is not time to waste; the
time is now. Do not look for tomorrow, for the
day of tomorrow is uncertain. You must grow
in Me now if you wish to share in My glory
which I offer to you, and gladly rejoice in
those who say "yes."*

* * *

Extract from a message to the Young Adults' Prayer Group, given by Mary, through Stefanie, September 6, 1991:

*It is with great joy that I welcome you and
that I renew my mission, my mission of love
and joy and peace and conversion. My dear
ones, I ask you now to rededicate all of your
hearts, all of your minds, all of your bodies,
and all of your lives to this mission. There
shall be many to care for in the name of my
Son. There shall be many to feed and to
strengthen, many to love and to comfort. My
dear children, I so need you, my strong and
youthful army, my courageous children, who
shall bring my banner, my banner of love, to
all the world.*

*My dear ones, know my Son, know Him in
your lives, know Him in your hearts, know
Him in your world. I know it is difficult at
times to be fully aware of His loving presence.
But this, my dear ones, is your task; to be*

fully aware, fully open, to the loving presence of your Lord, our God.

My dear children, I bless you and I thank you, and I ask you to rally in spirit toward the love of Our Lord, so you may become holy and blessed. Blessed is the child Jesus that He stretched out His arms to love and bless, to console; blessed is He. And it is through the arms of your loving mother that you are called. Please accept the call. Please accept the love, and know that I am with my Son in praise of the Triune God.

Stefanie

CHAPTER 8

Is It Real?

In October, 1989, a three person Commission of Inquiry named by the Bishop of Phoenix, Bishop Thomas O'Brien, submitted its report on the authenticity of the alleged events at Scottsdale. At the time of the commission's investigations, the "apparitions" during the Thursday night Rosary had not yet begun. But locutions were taking place; messages were being written down and stated.

The commission evaluated these locutions, or words allegedly received by Gianna, Stefanie, Annie, and Father Jack Spaulding, from the point of view of their supernaturality. Are they really from God and from the Mother of God, or not?

A Carmelite theologian well known in the field of spirituality, Father Ernest Larkin, resident in the diocese of Phoenix, acted as head of the commission. The other two members were Franciscan Sister Mary Therese Sedlock and James Lange, Ph.D.

The Commission of Inquiry concluded that the messages "are explainable within the range of ordinary human experience." The commission stated that, "obviously we cannot know for certain whether or not the locutions or visions are miraculous in the true sense of the word. By miraculous we mean a mode of action beyond the ordinary laws of nature and caused by an exceptional, direct divine intervention." The commission further found that "Father Spaulding has demonstrated himself to be a good priest and he should be commended for his devotion to Our Lady." The commitment to God and the deep faith of all the individuals involved were also pointed out.

These quotations come from Bishop Thomas O'Brien's official statement on the alleged apparitions published in the diocesan Catholic weekly newspaper, *The Catholic Sun,* of January 18, 1990. The report itself, as it was submitted to the bishop the previous October, has never been published. On the front page of the same issue, an article on the report quotes Father Larkin extensively.

"We don't think that these are hoaxes or that there is any attempt to deceive anybody. We simply maintain that there is not enough evidence to say that these are miracles. . .We're not saying that it's impossible that these are miracles, we're just saying that it's impossible to conclude that these are miracles."

Dr. Lange, a psychologist on the seminarian review board for the diocese, said that he had only a limited role on the Commission of Inquiry, and that he found nothing aberrant from a psychological point of view, and no indication of deceit. He added that those concerned have great faith.

Sister Mary Therese Sedlock manifested a pastoral concern that simple parishioners might put their faith in visions and messages rather than "just living a life of faith in the spirit of Jesus." About the young adults and Father Spaulding, she said, "I felt they lacked a certain openness."

Bishop Thomas O'Brien followed the findings of the commission and endorsed their recommendations:

"1. The prayer meetings and public devotions at Saint Maria Goretti Church may continue for the spiritual welfare of all concerned. There may not be,

however, any unequivocal claim of miraculous intervention. This is due to the absence of any external evidence that the messages are directly from Our Lord
Jesus Christ or the Blessed Virgin Mary.

"2. In order to maintain the unity of the prayer
group at Saint Maria Goretti Church with the whole
church, I am establishing a 'Community of Discernment.' The Community of Discernment will aid the
prayer group in interpreting any future events; direct
the development of devotion to Our Lady; monitor the
circulation of any publications produced by the prayer
group."

In fact, we could find no evidence of any Community
of Discernment ever having been established, nor of
any names of people who constitute the membership
of such a community. No one we spoke to in the parish
knew anything about it.

The "lack of openness" felt by Sister Mary Therese
Sedlock may be explained by looking from the point
of view of the nine intelligent young people. The commission, interviewing the nine together, asked them a
question: "If you could put into one word how this has
affected you, what word would you use?" Some said
"hope," some "trust," some "humility." But most
summed up their experience as one of peace, obedience and trust.

The commission members spoke to the nine for forty
minutes, chiefly explaining who they were and what
they did. "At the end of the interview" says one of the
nine, "they put their cards on the table and told us
that if there was anything that we thought they should
know in addition to what we had discussed at the
interview, we could call them and set up an interview;
that they could be reached at any time.

"We were all very hesitant thinking this was odd.
Then Jimmy spoke up and said, 'I don't think anyone

is going to do that. It is not our job to call you.' Stefanie added, 'You are the commission that was formed to investigate this, and, I mean no disrespect, but if you would like to reach any of us, you have our phone numbers and you have a way to get hold of us. Any one of us would be delighted to meet you at any time. Name the time and set up an appointment with any of us, and we will be happy to sit and talk with you.' They have never called us. None of us has called them."

Since October 1989 some things have changed. For one thing, apparitions have begun to take place regularly during the Rosary at the Thursday night prayer meeting. Annie and Gianna are clearly in some kind of ecstatic state during these alledged apparitions to them. This is an example of new evidence, and needs assessment. According to guidelines issued to all bishops by the Holy See, a preliminary investigation with at least somewhat positive results, like the investigation by the Commission of Inquiry in Scottsdale, needs follow-up by a more elaborate and extensive investigation. We can expect this to take place quite soon, unless of course the Vatican directives go ignored, which seems unlikely.

The Vatican guidelines for bishops in the matter of apparitions has the title, *Norms of the Sacred Congregation for the Doctrine of the Faith concerning How to Proceed in Judging Alleged Apparitions and Revelation.* The document, in Latin, confidential and for local bishops only, is dated February 25, 1978, and signed by the then head of the Sacred Congregation for the Doctrine of the Faith, Cardinal Seper. It describes investigative procedures, gives the positive and negative criteria for the use of the local bishop in evaluating religious apparitions in his jurisdiction, and states the conditions for interventions on the part of the Holy See and on the part of the National Conference of Bishops.

We have found these norms to be well balanced, concise, and useful. In an explanation of why these norms were promulgated when they were, the guidelines give reasons. Mass media today diffuse information about apparitions rapidly. Ease of travel facilitates pilgrimages. At the same time, bishops have difficulty in arriving at clear cut judgments quickly so as to forbid or to permit a public cult or other devotional practices at the place of the alleged apparitions. The ideal is to arrive at a judgment of supernaturality [in Latin: *constat de supernaturalitate*] or of non-supernaturality [*constat de non-supernaturalitate*]. Note that the judgment of the Scottsdale Commission of Inquiry, and of the bishop of Phoenix, was neither; it was a judgment that no decisive evidence of supernaturality could be found [*non constat de supernaturalitate*].

The Sacred Congregation for the Doctrine of the Faith stipulates three stages in a basic plan of investigative action to be followed by the local bishop.

Stage one: the local bishop and his representatives judge the facts according to positive and negative criteria.

Stage two: if the resulting judgment is favorable, as in the case of Scottsdale, the local bishop permits manifestations of public devotion and worship. He does this prudently, letting it be known that he finds no obstacle to such practices. Bishop O'Brien of Phoenix has done just that in his official statement published in the diocesan *Catholic Sun* in early 1990.

Stage three: in the light of the experience of healthy devotion and of spiritual fruit over a certain length of time, a judgment of truth and of supernaturality can be made. In fact, this frequently takes the form of naming the place as a shrine, or of a positive approval of devotion there, or both. This step has not been taken in Scottsdale.

What are the criteria of authenticity for apparitions? We can look at these and make our own application to the Scottsdale case.

Here are the positive criteria:
1. That, after a serious investigation, the facts are found to be as claimed, at least with a high degree of probability.
2. That the persons alleged to be having supernatural experiences be judged as psychologically and morally sound, honest and sincere, and with a respectful attitude toward church authority.
3. Further, any religious doctrine contained for example in messages must be free from error.
4. Finally, healthy religious devotion and spiritual fruits [for example a spirit of prayer, conversions] are positive signs.

These are the negative criteria:
1. There should be no obvious error about the facts.
2. No doctrinal errors should be attributed to Jesus or to Mary.
3. Money making should not have an important role in the events.
4. Evidence should not be found of gravely immoral acts on the part of the people having the alleged experiences, or of mental illness, or of collective hysteria or similar aberrations.

These criteria are indicative, they are not absolute. Usually, investigating commissions and the bishop have to make their judgments on the basis of converging lines of evidence.

We can apply these criteria easily to the Scottsdale apparitions. First of all, the basic facts are as claimed. At least three young women, Gianna, Annie, and Mary do claim to have apparitions, locutions, and very strong prophecies. One young woman, Stefanie, says she has locutions and prophecies. And the pastor, Father Spaulding, claims to somehow speak for Jesus and Mary at the Thursday night prayer meetings. Certainly, something is going on.

Secondly, as the Commission of Inquiry found, the faith and morals and psychological health of the people involved are quite sound; they all show great spiritual, moral, and psychological health. Thirdly, we can find no doctrinal error in any of the messages. Fourthly, positive signs do present themselves: conversions, and a spirit of prayer and devotion.

As to an application of the negative criteria: There is no obvious error about the facts. No doctrinal errors are attributed to Mary or to Jesus. There is no evidence of anyone making any money from the alleged phenomena. And there is no evidence of immoral acts on the part of those involved, nor of any mental illness, nor of collective hysteria nor of anything similar.

An application of the document of the Holy See, of its criteria for judging the authenticity of alleged apparitions, to Scottsdale, results in converging lines of evidence that do clearly point to a positive judgment. We do not speak here about believing or about not believing in the Scottsdale apparitions. The church teaches that we can believe in such apparitions as long as they are not condemned by the church. But we are not obliged to believe in them, even after church approval. Each one is, at every point, free to believe or not to believe. We speak here not about subjective belief, but, rather, about objective reality and about making a judgment on the evidence about what seems to be taking place in Saint Maria Goretti Parish in Scottsdale. And our judgment has to be that the Scottsdale apparitions certainly do seem to be real, to be authentic.

What about the possibility of an intervention from authorities higher than Bishop O'Brien of Phoenix? This does not seem at all likely, at least for the foreseeable future. The Vatican document provides for the possibility of an intervention of the National Conference of Bishops, especially if the local bishop asks for it, and for the possibility of intervention on the part of the Holy See, again especially if the bishop requests it. And of course the Vatican could intervene on its own, as it has done in the case of the Medjugorje apparitions in Yugoslavia. But there is no reason to think that the bishop of Phoenix will request such an intervention, nor to think that circumstances might provoke such an intervention.

In the meantime, the situation continues and evolves. Eventually, the bishop of Phoenix will have to make a further investigation and a further and more precise judgment.

Appendix

Note: The messages given to the parish, through Gianna Talone at the Thursday evening Adult Prayer Group, the Lessons (given by Jesus to Gianna Talone), and the homily messages given through Father Jack Spaulding at the Thursday night Masses have been published in two volumes, with a third volume published just prior to this book.

I Am Your Jesus of Mercy
Volume I (1989)
Volume II (1990)
Volume III (1991)

Published by:
The Riehle Foundation
P.O. Box 7
Milford, OH 45150

The messages which follow occurred after the publishing of the above referenced volumes.

Thursday Messages from the Blessed Virgin Mary

JULY 25, 1991: "My dear children, I can only ask you to love unconditionally, because my love for my Son is unconditional, and my hope is that you will hasten to His call. My dear little children, God loves you and only brings good tidings to you. He wishes to cleanse you with His truth and holiness. Be open to His call, and do your best every day to follow the only way, the way of my Son. Bless you my dear little ones! I bless you and wrap you in my mantle of prayer. Thank you for responding to my call of love."

AUGUST 1, 1991: "My dear children, I am your Mother of Grace who possesses all goodness from my Son. He wishes for you to live in his oneness of the Holy Trinity. Please, my dear children, do not delay in loving. There is little time to put aside love for your brethren. Turn to my Son and He will bestow on you the many graces of eternal life. Live in peace. Remember, without love there cannot be unity, and without unity there cannot be peace. LOVE, LOVE, LOVE my Son by loving one another. Praise be my Son! Bless you my children! And thank you for responding to my call."

AUGUST 8, 1991: "My dear children, I your Mother of Joy come to invite you again, to be little children of God. God does exist, my dear ones. Please be pure.

Have faith and trust in my Son. Fidelity to God will keep your hearts pure, and simplicity is the way. Seek always to please God by seeking to do His will. I bless you my dear little children; my children whom I bring to my Son. He will grace you abundantly. Keep your eyes fixed on Him in a true intimacy which He is seeking from you. Bless you my dear ones, and thank you for your response to my call."

AUGUST 22, 1991: "My dear children, I come to you because the grace of my Son has allowed His goodness to be shed upon all mankind. He desires you to be filled with His eternal blissful Spirit, and share in eternal happiness. *Please*, my dear children, unite in harmony and live peacefully. Allow your behavior to speak for the words of your actions. Be loving, and live in my Son's goodness. There is no time to shed wasteful energy when God has granted you the gift of love. I bless you my dear ones, and invite you once again to be committed to my Son in love. Thank you for responding to my call."

AUGUST 29, 1991: "My dear children, the grace of my Son does not present pressure. There is only peace with my Son. Be at peace and be calm in Him. Look to Him for comfort, and follow the truth in unity. Please my dear little children, God is good. Come to my Son like little children, child-like, joyful and carefree. Thank Him. How grateful and happy I am that He has allowed me the grace to be here with you. I bless you my little children and bring you my Son's peace. Thank you for responding to my call."

SEPTEMBER 5, 1991: "My dear children, live in simpleness. Simple ways and loving ways. Always seek to be calm, taking one day at a time. Oh, my children of God, blessed are you who follow in simpleness. Seek purity and live good, not bad, ways. I bless you this evening with the grace from God. Strive to be simple. My message is to love and to be simple. Do not try to understand. Simply live day by day in my Son's light. Thank you for responding to my call."

Friday Messages From the Young Adults' Prayer Group: Extracts

NOTE: The messages come from Jesus and from Our Lady. They usually come through Stefanie Staab, through Gianna Talone, or through Mary Cook, and sometimes through Annie Ross. Until now, these Friday evening messages have not been published. The Friday night messages differ from those given on Thursdays; they are not dictated, but inspired directly. They seem to be prophecies, messages inspired by the Holy Spirit, of a particularly strong and direct kind.

FROM OUR LADY ON JULY 28, 1989, GIVEN THROUGH STEFANIE: "Tonight there are many of you who I see are here for the first time. I thank you, my dear ones, for coming, and I welcome you. Children, it is a time of rejoicing this day. So many of you have worked so hard to open your hearts to God. . . . My dear sweet children, you must know how very much I love you. I will tell you this over and over as all mothers do their children, for I wish for you to have embedded in your hearts and in your souls the knowledge of my love which is my Son's love as well.

"I wish for each child here to look, for one full day only, at your progress. My dear ones, you must be encouraged by the steps that you, by my Son's grace, have been able to take, to step all that much closer to Him. Please make tomorrow a day for each of you to reflect on your progress along your spiritual path in the last year. So many have worked so hard. I have prayed to my Son that He show you the steps that you have made as He sees them.

"It is time for each of you to say 'thank you, thank you' to my Son Who has allowed me to come and Who has, in His mercy and in His love, honored my prayers as I requested that He bring to me more and more children so that we may come to rejoice in His love. I ask you, open yourselves to what He will show you. Take this time to be encouraged. Yes, my dear ones, there is still far to go. There always will be far to go until that day when we all sit together in my Son's paradise along with the Almighty God. But do not be discouraged by focusing solely on where you still must go. I ask you to rejoice and be glad and to give to my Son praise and thanksgiving. That is all, my children. Let your hearts rejoice."

FROM OUR LADY ON THE SAME DAY, JULY 28, 1989, GIVEN THROUGH STEFANIE: "My children, thank you for coming. Thank you for coming week after week with your hearts open to my Jesus, in devotion to Him and in dedication of your lives to Him. I thank you. I know you are weary and I thank you for first seeking my Son. Know you are all doing so very well. Thank you. You fill me with much joy. I am so pleased to present you to my Son and to offer your prayers to Him on your behalf. My dear ones, I ask of you now to listen closely. My children, do not be secretive. I speak to you to share my words, my heart, my love with you.

"Please share with one another. ... Help one another by sharing what you have heard or what you have experienced and what you have learned. ... Unless it has been made known to you to not mention anything that We have spoken for your benefit, then do not keep things secret. I am not a secret to you. My Son is not a secret to you. We are here for you and for every one of Our children. Do not be afraid of one another or of what you should say. Simply be the beautiful children you are, of your own character and personality, and share. . . . Our words are for everyone, and so I ask you to share. Thank you my dear ones, thank you very much. I love you dearly, and it is with great joy that I present your petitions to my Son Who will in turn present them to His Father, Our Father."

FROM JESUS ON THE SAME DAY, JULY 28, 1989, GIVEN THROUGH GIANNA: "My dear followers, thank you for being and for wanting to be My followers. I grant you My glory to live with Me in My oneness and in My kingdom. My dear ones, please persevere. I am guiding you. With time you will know and understand. . .

"I remind you, in your weariness once again to persevere in My strength and to continue working, and praying to My Father and to My most beloved mother. Perseverance will strengthen you in My faith. It will strengthen you in your faith.

"Dear ones, please heed the words My mother spoke to you. Do not be secretive. It hinders your growth. Many feel rejected when you do not share. Remember, I do not reject you, so do not reject others.

"Your prayers will not go unanswered. Know with all of your heart, as I speak to you, that I hear you and will answer you in accordance with My Father's will. I love you, My dear ones and thank you for your perseverance. Be grateful; the work that has been given to you is part of your growth, and I shall be your strength.

"I bless you this night in the name of My Father, in the name of My Spirit, in the name of My beloved mother whom I give to you. I bless you with her, and in My name I bless you My dear ones, My disciples who will live in My Faith. Go out and bear much fruit and live My gospel words. All of My people; peace to you."

FROM JESUS ON AUGUST 4, 1989, GIVEN THROUGH GIANNA: "My dear children, it is I your Lord Who come to you this night. I come with many greetings. I come with greetings of love and of joy and of hope. Hope in you, hope in all of you gathered here and in those who gather here with you each week.

"My dear ones, it is time; it is time for you to decide once again the degree to which you will commit to My work that I want to be done through My dear mother. Do you understand the love between My mother and Me? So many do not understand this love, so many find it so difficult to believe that so much glory, so much honor, should be bestowed upon a person by God as is bestowed upon My mother. Do not allow these doubts to sadden your hearts. Seek, My dear ones, and you will find. Seek the knowledge of My mother's relationship with Me and with Our eternal Father. It will inspire you and help you to see why you have been selected to assist My mother who assists Me. I ask you to seek this knowledge so that you may better understand.

"My dear children, I love and I call you, to be apostles of My love and of My mercy. Do you understand what an apostolate is? It is carrying My words and My love and mercy to all those that you meet. You need not be scholarly or sinless. So many are discouraged by the sins that they see in themselves. Realize that all of My apostles throughout time had sin of some sort within them. It has not stopped Me from selecting you, do not allow it to stop you from selecting Me or My work. The time will come when many will be brought here. I ask you to prepare yourselves. Fast, pray, follow My mother's words and instruction. It is she who taught Me when I was a child, and so now she will teach you. Know that you are so tremendously graced in this age with her presence, and be thankful.

As I tell you that I am happy with the strides that

each of you is making, I must also encourage you to go on, push forward, strive harder. . . . I encourage you, children, for I need you close to My heart. My mother rejoices, and in her joy I have joy. Feel good about the strides you are making, but know the source of your power. . . . Glory to Our Father in Heaven! Amen, My dear ones, amen."

FROM OUR LADY ON AUGUST 11, 1989, GIVEN THROUGH STEFANIE: ". . .There are many things I wish to prepare you for, many, many things that I wish to bring into your lives. So much joy, and peace, and purpose, you will have. You have been so faithful to me. I have called you, and you have fought your pride, your envy, your selfishness, the things of the world; and, my children, how you have grown. You have grown in love and charity, in peace and in faith. . . . I want to encourage you and thank you. . . .

"My dear ones, how happy I am. It is almost a year now that you have come to me, hearing my words and the words of my Son and seeking Him and allowing Him to change your hearts, to cleanse your souls, and to bring you closer and closer to happiness. Thank you so very much. The bliss of Heaven shall be yours. So many will look to you, my dear ones. They will come seeking guidance and encouragement, and you will be ready. I look back to when you first came, not knowing what this meant in your life, being fearful, being skeptical. I look back, and then I look at you now and I am filled with such joy. You must be at peace, my dear ones, with the knowledge that you are growing in my Son's grace every day. . . .

"Wait in joy and hope, for soon you will be more active as my army who will bring my Son's love to so very many people. Bless you my dear ones, I love you and I thank you. Amen."

FROM OUR LADY ON OCTOBER 19, 1990, GIVEN THROUGH STEFANIE: "My dear ones, I your mother am here with you, praying with you. My dear ones, I am here, and I am praying with you. This night it is my Son's desire to address you, so I am here simply praying with and for you. I have taken your petitions to my most Immaculate Heart, and I will comfort you in my mantle and offer you to the eternal Father for His blessings. May your desires always be His desires, and may you unite with Him in union and oneness. May you live in His peace and in His beauty and in His strength. I love you, my dear blessed children! Know that I am here this night with you!"

FROM JESUS, THE SAME NIGHT, OCTOBER 19, 1990, GIVEN THROUGH GIANNA: "My dear children, how I await your love. Know that it is My desire to come this night to you to make known My love for each one of you.

"My dear beloved one, I, your Lord Jesus, await your love. Pray for detachment, My dear ones, detachment from the world, yet longing for Mine.

"I wish to give you many graces, yet you must know that you are powerless. It is I that give to you even in your desire to follow Me. It is I that give you the grace to make the decision of your free will. It is I that give you grace and strength of prayer and growth. It is I Who am guiding you.

"Please be comfortable in your journey, for where you are is where I desire you to be. Even your struggles I allow, for it is in your struggles and in your imperfections that you grow in humility.

"My dear ones, tonight I want you to know that I have not abandoned you; I am following you. I am by you. I am leading you! Yet, you must surrender to Me. . . . It is I Who know each one of you and what you need.

"Please be open to Me or you will deceive yourself. I love you, it is no secret. Yet you try to be secretive even with Me. Be open! Even though I know what you are hiding, what joy it gives Me when you come open-hearted and share with Me all your imperfections, which I have allowed. . . .

"Your desire is My desire. Now pray that My desire is always your desire. I bless you and I keep you. You are safe, so be at peace, My peace with blessings from My Father.

FROM OUR LADY, FEBRUARY 2, 1991, GIVEN THROUGH STEFANIE: ". . .Tonight, my dear ones, I shall speak of faith, faith in daily living. You see, my dear ones, it is one thing to have faith in prayer, to have faith in spiritual reading, to have faith in the traditions and teachings of the Church, and in my Son's Word. But it is another to have faith in daily living; the faith that lets you not forget that each part of your day is held by my Son, to bring about the greatest good for your soul.

"Often times, my children wonder why they are employed in a certain vocation, in a certain work or place, or with people who are unpleasant to them. They often wonder 'Why are there not more friends in my life? Why are there not others in my life who I would desire to spend more time with?' They often wonder, 'Why am I not having fun? Why must I work? Why must I serve? Why must I be compassionate to those who are a drain on me, on what I wish to do for my life?'

"These questions will be answered by faith, faith in my Son Who guides your day, Who guides your minutes and Who guides your very life. He creates for you situations that will cause you to learn holiness, to learn mercy and to learn love.

"My dear ones, when, because of your life situations, you face a circumstance or a task which you do not find pleasant or fun or carefree, embrace the cross of my Son, and have faith in it.

"Do not embrace it as a martyr, dreading what is about to come. Embrace it as a martyr who rejoices in repenting and in sacrifice, for they know in the depths of their hearts that they are walking with Our Lord..."

FROM OUR LADY, JULY 19, 1991, GIVEN THROUGH MARY COOK: "My dear ones, it brings me such joy to see you faithfully pray to my Son. I welcome you in my arms this night, into my holy mantle. I give you my peace and my love.

"You are so special to me, my children. Please pray, pray with all your hearts, to be true to my Son, to overcome your faults and to practice patience and humility with your brothers and sisters. Trust in God, my dear ones, trust in Him. He loves you so much. He will not do anything to hurt you. Know that He is with you always, and I am with Him, holding your hand, leading you to salvation! Peace be with you, my little ones. Pray. Pray!"

FROM OUR LADY, GIVEN AUGUST 9, 1991, THROUGH MARY COOK: "My dear ones, I am so happy to be with you tonight. Tonight I wish to talk with you about faith in my Son. Have faith, children. Have faith that He is taking care of you. Trust in His will for you. By faith, you are loving my Son. You are allowing Him to take control over your life. When you take control, children, it leads to much confusion and anxiety. Please, please allow Him to do His will in you. Pray, pray that His will be done. Have faith and trust, my little ones. My peace is with you always."

FROM JESUS, GIVEN AUGUST 16, 1991, THROUGH MARY COOK: "My dear ones, what will it take for you to believe in Me, for you to trust Me completely with your life? I do love you so. I still suffer because of lack of trust. I'm guiding you, My dear ones. I'm guiding you back to Me. *Please* trust Me. Pray, pray with all your heart before it's too late. Come *back* to Me My dear ones [weeping]. The kingdom of Heaven is yours to take. It is your choice. Follow My path. I your Lord will never lead you wrong. Follow My mother. She will lead you to Me. Love one another children. Love. "I love you! I love you so."

FROM OUR LADY, AUGUST 23, 1991, THROUGH GIANNA: "My dearest children, I, your mother, come tonight thanking you for your prayers, inviting you to my Son. Oh my dear beloved ones, how I praise my Son, your Lord Jesus. Go to Him and worship in praise and in simpleness. He is your Lord of mercy, your Lord of compassion, your Lord of joy, your Lord of hope, your Lord of faith.

"Oh my dear children, He is so good, and He invites you to live in the Oneness of the Holy Trinity in His kingdom. He invites you to simpleness, to live in purity.

"My dear, dear children, seek to please Him always in simpleness. SET ASIDE YOURSELF, AND GAIN LIFE! He is your everything. With Him you can only accomplish everything.

"Faith is not a feeling, my dear ones, it is a fact; and my Son has come there to shed His mercy, to gather His flock and to guide them. He is the Way, and He wishes for you to live His Way. There is much to say, and such little time!

"Know that my Son has allowed me to come here. It is a grace. Set aside your childish ways. Take seriously my Son's Way. His Way is not foolish! His Way is Life!

"There is so much hope, my dear ones. I can only plead with you to go before Him in humility. You are all so very dear, and so very graced by my Son. Blessed be His holy name, for He has given you to me, and you my dear ones are so very blessed.

"Let us now pray for perseverance. I bless you, my dear ones; but above all the Father, the Creator, blesses you. NEVER LOSE SIGHT OF HIM, FOR WITHOUT HIM YOU CANNOT SEE!'"

FROM JESUS, THE SAME NIGHT, AUGUST 23, 1991, THROUGH GIANNA: "I, your sweet Jesus of Mercy, come before you to ask you, 'What is it that man can give you that I cannot give?'

"My dear ones, so many worries and anxieties that you have are those that you create. It is not that I give them to you. It is that you live in a world of anxiety; but I have come to conquer the world. So you see, My dear ones, if you focus on Me, you can only live in peace; but mind you: the peace that I have established, peace by God's standards, not peace by man's standards.

"With peace comes change. With peace, there can be inner conflict! I call you to a pure way, the only way.

"There are many seats in My kingdom, a seat for you. I have said, 'Come, come to Me.' Come and ask Me questions, but come before Me when you have questions, not when you have worries!

"Oh My dear beloved disciples, do not be afraid of change. Live in My strength. Take the risk to follow My way.

"Words are only words, so when man speaks, what do you seek? Acceptance of words? Or do you live for acceptance of Me? Time after time I have told you; I have pleaded with you; I have died for you and I live for you. And I continually bear My wounds for you because of My love for you, because of the love My Father bears for you, a love some day you shall totally embrace.

"As I bless each of you in this room and as I bless

all My people in the world, I can only invite you and pray for you, for you are free.

"I have said, 'What you hold bound shall be bound.' I can only ask you to 'let it go!' My Way is simple, perhaps difficult because of change, but change for good and change for pure happiness and pure joy and pure inner peace.

"My Way is simple, so be free!

"As the birds are free that soar through the air, you are free, if only you allow your soul to soar, with Me! I love you. I'm here for you. I am devoted and committed to you.

"Please decide yes or no. Do not fluctuate back and forth. There are only two ends. There is no middle.

"Peace. Peace as My Father has granted peace and strength. I live for you in love. . ."

THE
RIEHLE
FOUNDATION...

The Riehle Foundation is a non-profit, tax-exempt, charitable organization that exists to produce and/or distribute Catholic material to anyone, anywhere.

The Foundation is dedicated to the Mother of God and her role in the salvation of mankind. We believe that this role has not diminished in our time, but, on the contrary has become all the more apparent in this the era of Mary as recognized by Pope John Paul II, whom we strongly support.

During the past four years the foundation has distributed books, films, rosaries, bibles, etc. to individuals, parishes, and organizations all over the world. Additionally, the foundation sends materials to missions and parishes in a dozen foreign countries.

Donations forwarded to The Riehle Foundation for the materials distributed provide our sole support. We appreciate your assistance, and request your prayers.

IN THE SERVICE OF JESUS AND MARY
All for the honor and glory of God!

The Riehle Foundation
P.O. Box 7
Milford, OH 45150